PASTORAL PSYCHIATRY

PASTORAL PSYCHIATRY

By

John Sutherland Bonnell

with a Foreword by
Thaddeus Hoyt Ames, M.D.

HARPER & BROTHERS PUBLISHERS

New York   London

To

MY FATHER

CONTENTS

Foreword

Pastoral Psychiatry is a title which fittingly describes this book. Dr. Bonnell points out that the word *psychiatry*, according to its derivation and the usage of the Bible, pertains primarily to the soul and secondarily to the mind. As a pastor, in his work with individuals he directs his efforts as definitely and directly to the cure of souls as medical psychiatrists direct theirs to the regulation of feelings, emotions, and thoughts. He is a pastoral psychiatrist.

The descriptions of typical conversations with parishioners and his ways of dealing with their problems indicate that he has what a casual observer might consider a technique of psychotherapy—i.e., a therapy to the mind, but which a close observer will see is therapy to the soul.

This book with its contents and implications may well be the forerunner of great achievement, both spiritually for individuals and for peoples, and technically for any and all therapists who work with human problems. It extends beyond the horizon of medical psychiatry both in its manifest and in its latent content, and has in it what pastors of any denomination ought and want to know and use in their daily work with parishioners.

It also demonstrates the belief that spiritual health and activity produce not only mental health, freedom, and happiness in a secular sense, but also the abundant life.

THADDEUS HOYT AMES, M.D.

New York City
October, 1938

ix

Introduction

My usage of the word *psychiatry* differs from the prevailing usage sufficiently for me to draw attention to the origin of the word.

It is derived from the two Greek words ψυχή, *psyche,* and ιατρεία, *iatreia.* The usual translation of the former, "mind," happens to be not the primary meaning of the word but the third in the order in Liddell and Scott's Greek Lexicon. There the word is defined in the following order:

I. "Breath, especially as the sign of life, life, spirit."

II. "The soul of man, as opposed to the body."

III. "The soul, mind, reason, understanding."

These Greek words, ψυχή, "soul" or "mind," and ιατρεία, "healing," "medical treatment," when combined have come to mean "treatment of the mind" and have been used by both laity and the medical profession either explicitly or implicitly to apply to the therapy for mental disease by physicians. So exclusively has the word been used for medical men that no lay therapist calls himself psychiatrist.

Anyone interested in the origins of words is accustomed to accept the order of listing of definitions by an authority so competent as "Liddell and Scott."

The first and second definitions of the word *psyche—viz.,* breath, life, spirit, soul of man—all have to do, *not* with the fundamentals of medicine, which is found in the third meaning, *viz.,* the mind, reason, understanding, but have to do with the essence of religion.

The word *psychiatry* then means primarily "the healing of the soul of man," as opposed not only to the body, but also to the mind, reason, and understanding.

In a recording of Jesus' conversation with the scribe who asked Him which is the first commandment in the law, the Master replied, "Thou shalt love the Lord thy God with all thy heart, and with all thy soul, and with all thy mind, and with all thy strength: this is the first commandment."[1]

In the Greek Testament in three Gospels[2] the word for "soul" is ψυχή; for "mind" is διάνοια, *dianoia*. Jesus definitely made a distinction between the words.

I am following the New Testament interpretation of the word *psyche* in this book. I do this having a life-long awareness of the medical connotations of the word, but with my equally long intimacy with the application of spiritual healing to the soul. I do not consider myself a psychiatrist as physicians are psychiatrists. My work differs from that of the physician and psychiatrist in that my resources and goals are primarily spiritual. I seek God's help with the problem at hand.

Throughout this book I have deliberately refrained, wherever possible, from using technical medical, psychiatric and theological terms and phraseology.

The identity of all persons who have consulted me is fully concealed in this book by the use of fictitious names and by a slight alteration in revealing details of no psychiatric or spiritual significance.

[1] St. Mark XII:30.
[2] St. Matthew XXII:37. St. Mark XII:30. St. Luke X:27.

I. *My Father*

"Well done, thou good and faithful servant: thou hast been faithful over a few things, I will make thee ruler over many things: enter thou into the joy of thy lord."

—St. Matthew xxv:21

"Peace I leave with you, my peace I give unto you: not as the world giveth, give I unto you. Let not your heart be troubled, neither let it be afraid."

—St. John xiv:27

"I will fear no evil: for thou art with me."

—Psalm xxiii:4

For forty-six years my father was a member of the staff of Falconwood Hospital, Charlottetown, Prince Edward Island. During the greater part of that time he was supervisor of this mental institution. From the age of ten it was my great delight to spend occasional weekends with him in his apartment there. Often he took me along when he made his morning rounds. He carried a basket of dressings on his arm, ready for certain patients assigned him by the physician. In one of the wards he would turn to me and say,

"You may stay here with the attendant. I have some ugly dressings to do in another ward."

While waiting for him I spent the time chatting with the patients and listening to their conversation. They were friendly to me and accepted me as part of my father.

During those early years I learned to recognize, in a rudimentary fashion, the various types of mental illness. Technical terms and fuller understanding came later.

There was Jimmie, forty-five years of age, with the mentality of a child. I never tired of listening to him as he stood in a corner, at my request, and recited "Mary Had a Little Lamb." The patients called him to his face "Jimmie the idiot," but my father always called him "Jimmie."

Then there were the patients who suffered from various types of mania. One was Mike, an Irishman, whom I learned to know at this time and who was a good friend of mine during the following twenty-five years. It was very entertaining to listen to his droll wit and he enjoyed having an appreciative audience. This man was periodically a patient in the institution. He would remain from three to six months for treatment and would then be discharged. He was a mate on a sailing-vessel and oftentimes would enjoy a year or two of complete

3

sanity. Generally he became aware of the approach of an attack and would hasten back by himself to the hospital. Usually he reached it before the mental illness had completely mastered him.

When I saw him for the first time in the ward Mike was suffering from severe burns on his face and hands. On this occasion he had not started back to the hospital early enough. On his way he stopped off at a little town and, as he was a Roman Catholic, he attended Mass at the chapel there. Before going to church it occurred to him that he ought to offer a sacrifice to God at the service to supplement the work of the priest. Having come to this decision, he made plans accordingly. The ushers at the door of the church noticed this thick-set, well-dressed, kindly-looking man enter with a fairly large parcel under his arm. He took his place in the body of the church. At the climax of the Mass, when the attention of all the people was concentrated on what was occurring at the altar, he opened up his parcel and took out a large sheet that had been saturated with kerosene oil. Quickly he threw this over his head and set a match to it. The startled congregation saw a sheet of flame go up from one of the pews and, before the fire was extinguished the man had been severely burned. When I talked to him about this incident, he passed it off as a huge joke on himself. My father commented:

"I hope you realize by this time, Mike, that there are better ways for you to express your gratitude to God than by inflicting suffering on yourself."

One of the saddest men in the hospital was a melancholy Scotsman who patted me on the head and expressed the hope that I would never be so unfortunate as to come to a place like that institution. Then, as he talked, tears came to his eyes and he wept as he told me that his wife and children had died. Afterwards my father told me this was not true, though he said I should not think of the man as lying. He added that no useful purpose was served by my being upset at this man's distress. I noticed he did not wish me to stay very long with melancholia patients.

Over to one side, as immovable as a stake, lost in contemplation of his own visions, stood Bert. Each time I walked with my father near this patient, he would say: "Bert, my son has come to see you again." But Bert paid no attention to me. The expression of his face never changed. He did not move a muscle of his body. He never addressed a word to me or gave a sign that he noticed my coming or going. My father said that Bert treated him the same way. He always stopped and spoke to him, nevertheless, as he believed that he understood some of what was said to him, even though he did not respond. He added that Bert seemed to have a lot of thoughts and fantasies which were too deep for anyone to fathom. Years later my father described him as a case of dementia præcox.

I shall always remember an entertaining old sea captain who was possessed by a compulsive neurosis. When the whistle blew for dinner, as he left the ward with the rest of the patients he always touched certain doors, window casings, and benches on his way to the dining-hall. On one occasion I called the attention of an attendant to this odd characteristic. The keeper laughed and said, "You watch him now."

Just as the captain was approaching a bench which he was accustomed to touch, the attendant grappled with him and pulled him past the object, but the old captain struggled vigorously until he got free and, running back, placed his hand on the bench and then went his way quite happily.

My father said that this patient could have been cured if some one had understood him when he was younger, but that now he should not be at large even though his intelligence was not affected. His behaviour was too bizarre for a general public's peace.

I shall never forget my first visit to the "queen" who reigned in a female ward in this institution. My father said to me one day, when I was spending a weekend with him, "Would you like to meet the 'queen'?" On my giving a ready assent, he took me to Ward One in the female wing of the hospital. Having entered the long ward, we went directly to the room where the "queen" held her receptions.

My father knocked on the door and a quiet voice said, "Come in."

When we entered, I found that the patient had stood her bed on end, with the legs pointing to the wall and the iron bedstead projecting out into the room. The mattress was folded neatly away in the corner and covered with blankets. The "queen" was seated on a chair set directly on the lower bedstead, with the upper part over her head. Pillow shams and colored blankets were arrayed above her to form a canopy. All the fingers of her hands were covered with flashy rings such as one would purchase at a modern five-and-ten-cent store.

"Your Majesty," said my father, "may I present my son?"

"You may, indeed," she answered graciously and beckoned me to come forward.

"I shall be happy," she said, "to include you among my subjects, but I shall expect you always to obey my commands. Some day I shall make you a knight if you have proved obedient." Then, turning to my father, she said:

"I want you to see that a pail of candies is given to this young man and, when the pail is being filled, make sure that the servants do not touch the candies with their hands. Have them use a scoop."

The bearing of the woman was impressively regal. After a brief interview, my father asked permission for us to retire. During all the conversation there was a twinkle in his eyes, of which the "queen" was, of course, quite unaware. She always looked forward to his visits and regarded him as one of her most faithful subjects. When we were leaving she said to me, "My boy, I hope that some day you may be as good a man as your father."

In the middle of the afternoon, when walking through the hallway near the female wing, I suddenly came upon the "queen" down upon her knees on the floor, vigorously wielding a scrubbing-brush. I learned a truth that day which I have seen illustrated many times since. In one mind two separate and contradictory ideas may be held, but, because of dissociation, they are not allowed to confront each other in the individual's consciousness. In mental hospitals, therefore, a woman may be both "queen" and scrubwoman and a man may be at one and the same time "Ruler of the Universe" and an expert polisher of floors.

Years later, when I talked over the case of the "queen" with my father, he pointed out that the dissociation which enabled this woman to be both "queen" and scrubwoman is often manifested in less extreme forms in everyday life. He cited the instance of a man who was a pillar of orthodoxy in a certain church, but who, at the same time, was guilty of sharp practices in his business.

On only one occasion of all my visits to the institution as a boy did I have a really disturbing experience. I was about twelve years of age at the time. My father was detained in the wards by the serious illness of two patients and he had sent me to bed alone at nine o'clock. About midnight I woke up with a start, feeling that something was seriously amiss. As I sat up in bed in the dimly lighted room, there broke upon my ears the most unearthly sound I have ever heard. It was a low moan increasing in volume until it became a terrifying wail that rose higher and higher and then gradually died away. After about a minute's silence, the cry rang out again on the still night air. I sat on the bed with teeth chattering and limbs trembling, almost paralyzed with fear. How long I sat listening to those awful cries I cannot say, but to me it seemed an eternity. With immense relief I heard, at last, my father's footsteps in the hallway and the rattle of keys as he unlocked the bedroom door. He was greatly distressed at finding me awake and trembling with terror.

"Don't be frightened, son," he said in quiet, reassuring tones. "That's only John. You may remember seeing him yesterday working in the kitchen. This is the first bad attack he has had in weeks."

"What is the matter with him now?" I asked. "Is he in pain?"

"Not exactly," answered my father. "He believes, however, that he is being tortured. He says that we have a machine in this institution that he calls 'The Torch of the World,' and that we turn on some kind of an electric current that causes him to be filled with millions of needle pricks."

As I listened to the quiet voice of my father and learned the origin of the cries, I began to wonder why I had been afraid.

"You need not be ashamed of your fear," my father added, as though divining my thoughts, "because even grown-up attendants are terrified by these cries when they hear them for the first time. I am sorry this should have happened while I was away."

Later I became acquainted with John. He always appeared to be perfectly sane until he began to talk about his own case. Then he would tell me of the long years of persecution and torture he had undergone at the hands of his enemies. Whenever he saw two people talking together, he felt that they were plotting against him. My father explained that he was a paranoic. He said that we must all expect to be talked about by the members of our family and acquaintances and that, if we become too sensitive and suspicious regarding the opinion of us held by others, it clearly reveals something within us that needs correction.

As supervisor of the institution, it was part of my father's work to have oversight of the help in the hospital, to purchase supplies, to direct the attendants and patients who were responsible for keeping the roads, lawns, and trees of the hospital grounds in good order, in addition to innumerable duties in the oversight of the patients' well-being.

My father never attended college and had little intramural class attendance in addition to the course of lectures given by the medical superintendent. He read widely, however, in textbooks on psychiatry. His lack of academic training had no noticeable effect on his work, for the whole world was to him a school. The insane and sane, in and out of hospital, were the scholars and teachers.

My father was a close observer of what went on about him. He was constantly learning and he unceasingly gave forth to others what he had gleaned from life. He gave of himself without stint in the institution. He went on duty at 8 A.M. and left his office at 10 P.M. daily. He was off duty every second Sunday and each Tuesday afternoon, but he spent the greater part of these afternoons making purchases for the institution. In all his forty-six years in the hospital he had taken a holiday on not more than five occasions.

My father manifested inherent ability in taking care of people, whether they had wounds, lacerations, bruises, fractured bones, minds distorted by insanity, by immorality, by bad business or social judgment, or by sin. He was not only permitted, but also expected, by the physician to attend to patients in the hospital who needed surgical treatment.

It was always interesting to see him come into a ward. No sooner had he entered than there was a concerted movement of the patients towards him. It was as if they had been awaiting his coming. They came forward to shake his hand. As he walked through the corridors, I have seen him extend his hands towards the patients so that each of his fingers was held by a patient and his arms were gripped by others; so usually a group of patients walked along with him. They reminded one of little children, each of whom wishes to get as close as possible to his father. He would speak a word of French to a Frenchman, a sentence or two in Gaelic to a Highlander; he was "all things unto all men"; he reassured some, encouraged some, and stimulated others. He called each of them by his first name. He evidenced towards these patients the same courtesy and consideration that a doctor in a general hospital extends to the normal and the sane. He always listened carefully to what they had to say and treated their opinions with evident respect, speaking an encouraging word to them all.

I have seen him, on many occasions, go to the bedroom of a disturbed patient who was shouting and cursing. Without a moment's hesitation he would unlock the door and enter the room. Soon the patient sat quietly on the bed. My father either stood beside him or sat alongside him. He would talk to the patient about matters that were troubling him and would leave him, at the end of half an hour, greatly comforted with his mind at rest.

He made a practice of carrying a supply of tobacco cut into small pieces in his pockets and frequently he would distribute these to patients in the ward. On one occasion this habit very probably saved his life.

One evening, after nine o'clock, he was making a round of all the wards, as he frequently did. Lights were out and all the patients were locked in their rooms and dormitories. As he was passing through Ward Six he heard a terrific commotion coming from a dormitory where a dozen men slept. These patients were commonly regarded as harmless. Hurrying to the dormitory, he unlocked the door and looked in. There was sufficient light in the room for him to see that a battle was taking place. At that moment a giant of a man, who stood well over six feet in height and weighed some two hundred and fifty pounds, was beating another over the head with a galvanized pail. Blood was streaming down the faces of several other men who had previously been attacked. Just as my father entered the room, the big man, whose name was Tom, turned and started for the door, swinging the pail menacingly over his head. Before my father had a chance to retreat and lock the door from the outside, the man was on him. Something had to be done and done quickly, because the patient, with his great bulk and his enormous strength, was far more than a match for my father. In the very moment that the pail was swung into the air over my father's head, he reached quickly into his pocket and drew out three-quarters of a plug of chewing-tobacco and, addressing the enraged patient, said:

"Here, Tom, I have brought you this fig of tobacco." Momentarily the man hesitated. The pail remained suspended in the air for a second and then was lowered to the floor as Tom reached out greedily for the tobacco.

In that instant of crisis my father had remembered that this patient was possessed by an overpowering desire for tobacco and, acting swiftly on this recollection, he saved himself and the patients in the room from a severe if not a fatal beating.

No sooner had Tom taken the fig of tobacco than he bit off a huge piece of it with great satisfaction.

"Now, Tom," my father said, "I expect you to be a good boy since I brought you this tobacco. Go to your bed and I will spread the blankets over you."

Quietly the man obeyed. A few moments later the night watchman came through the ward and my father proceeded to dress the wounded.

Without any further trouble Tom was led quietly to another room where, thereafter, he slept alone.

My father used to say that one of the first principles that must be borne in mind by all who deal with the insane is that, in most cases, they should not cross the patient's delusions. He added that this does not apply, of course, to delusions that are intensely distressing or are dangerous to the life of the patient, or are a threat to the safety of other people. But even in the case of dangerous delusions, great care must be taken that the violent opposition of the patient be not aroused. It is futile to attempt to change the patient's mind in the case of his harmless delusions, because no argument can be produced that will convince him he is in error. He is positive, beyond all shadow of doubt, that he is right.

My father often pointed out the determination with which sane people sometimes hold mistaken ideas, and said that this was multiplied a thousandfold in the case of the insane. He said that a great deal can be done with the mentally afflicted if we work along the line of his delusion, not necessarily giving full assent to it, but moving in parallel lines of thought. Thus we may lead the patient to a conclusion that will put his mind at rest.

A striking illustration of this is seen in the case of Albert. He had shown considerable improvement and was, therefore, allowed to go out with the men who were working on the farm half a mile from the institution. One day, however, Albert suddenly threw to the ground the hoe with which he had been working and rushed from the turnip-field to an old well that had been filled in with stone and rubbish. Frantically he commenced hurling out the stones with his hands and digging ever deeper into the abandoned well. The attendant in charge of the patients said:

"What's the matter, Albert? What are you doing there?"

"Can't you hear them?" the man replied. "They've buried my two sons down in this well—buried them alive. Can't you hear them? I tell you they're crying to me for help."

The attendant tried to explain to Albert that the well had been filled with rubbish for years and that there could not, by any possibility, be anybody buried in its depths. Without stopping for a moment in his frantic labours, Albert cried:

"What's the use in your talking like that? I can hear them, I tell you. I can hear them calling to me."

Persuasion having failed, the attendant tried, with the assistance of another patient, to get Albert out of the well, but the man fought fiercely until he was put under restraint and conducted back to the institution.

When this incident was reported to my father, he visited Albert in the ward and found him in terrible agitation. His face was bleeding where he had torn it with his nails, before he had been put into a restraining jacket. He was sobbing piteously and pleading for somebody to go to the help of his boys.

"You will help me, Mr. Bonnell. I know you will help me. You will get the men to dig down into that well and save my boys."

Gently my father eased him into a chair and, sitting beside him, said:

"Now, Albert, you trust me, don't you?"

"Yes," the patient answered. "You're the only one I trust here."

"Well, if you trust me and believe I will do my best to help you, you must help me, too. It will do no good if you keep on getting more excited and crying like this. If you calm yourself and sit here, I promise to do my best for the safety of your boys and to bring you back word that they are both alive and well. Now, will you do your part by waiting quietly?"

Albert made the promise and my father left the ward.

Having gone to the office, he called up Albert's home by long-distance telephone and talked with one of his sons. He learned that the other boy was at home and got from him a message to give to the father.

In the interim, Albert sat with his eyes fastened upon the door of the ward, eagerly watching for my father's return. He heard the rattle of keys and hurried towards the door. My father stepped in briskly and, walking up to the patient, he said:

"Good news, Albert, good news! Your boys are safe and in a short time they will both be home. Your son George told me to tell you that they are going to start next week building that dairy that you always wanted. He said that he knew you would be pleased to hear this. You will get a letter from each of them tomorrow."

The old man's eyes lighted up with relief and joy as he heard this message. It was evident that he was convinced of the safety of his boys. Before he left the ward my father removed the restraining jacket from Albert and the patient was seated at the table, writing a letter to his sons.

It was interesting to hear my father talk about his patients. They were his children. He understood them and he loved them and his greatest joy was continually to minister to their every need.

The closing weeks of his life revealed the same concern for his patients that characterized his attitude for forty-six years. He had been seriously ill for almost a month. At last he was able to be up and around before the final and fatal attack. His first thought was for his patients and he made the rounds of several wards to see individuals who especially needed his attention, even though, at the time, he was so weak that he could hardly stand.

One man, in particular, was a source of a great deal of trouble to the institution. He was a farmer and a man of tremendous physical strength. He had the delusion that he had been placed in the institution by his relatives in order that they might secure his property. While my father was well, there had been little trouble with him because he unfailingly observed all his instructions, but during my father's absence from the institution for a month, this man became convinced that the supervisor had been killed because of his friendship with him. He was extremely violent and had to be kept constantly in a restraining jacket, as he had severely beaten two of the attendants. But worst of all, he went on a hunger strike and had to be forcibly fed because he claimed that they were trying to poison him.

He was the first patient to be visited by my father during his short reprieve from illness. The patient gave him a great welcome. My father said:

"I am sorry, Arthur, that you have not been eating your meals. Now I want you to have a good dinner and I have ordered them to bring it up to you now. You must be very hungry."

"You don't know what it means," the patient replied, "to have you back again. I thought they had done away with you."

The dinner was brought and my father fed it to the patient because he was still bound in the straitjacket. He was too dangerous to be freed.

When he had finished his dinner, my father said:

"Now, Arthur, I want you to take your meals regularly and I have asked this attendant to bring them to you and to feed you." He indicated the ward attendant who stood by.

Suddenly a look of suspicion came into the eyes of the man and he began very intently to study my father's face. Finally he said:

"Do you know, Mr. Bonnell, that I am beginning to wonder whether you stayed away on purpose so that these people might persecute me, and I am very doubtful whether I am going to eat any more meals or not. Look at the way they have tied me up. Do you think that is fair? Now, if you are my friend, I am soon going to know it because I want you to unloose this jacket and set me free. If you don't do that, I will know that you have joined with my enemies and I will not eat another bite."

My father related this incident to me at the hospital during his last illness. He said:

"I am quite frank to admit that for a moment I did not know what to say to him. I knew that if his suspicions were aroused against me he would resume his hunger strike and this would eventually mean his death. Suddenly an idea occurred to me, I said: 'Come over to the corner of the room for a minute,' and I drew him aside out of the hearing of the attendant. 'Now,' I continued, 'what was it that you told me your enemies are wanting you to do?'

" 'They put me in here to get my property,' he said, 'and every day they ask me to sign papers so that they will have me in their power.' " (This, of course, was purely a delusion.)

My father bent over him and whispered in his ear:

"Now listen to me. It would be a great mistake if I were to take that jacket off you, because that would ruin everything. When they come in again and ask you to sign those papers, say to them, 'I have this jacket on. Do you see how my hands are fastened? I cannot sign any papers.' "

The idea was immediately accepted by the patient and, from that day onward, he readily took food while still remaining in restraint.

I have always been impressed by the way in which my father dealt with the sane as well as the insane. He used to say: "Anybody who learns to deal happily with the insane should have little trouble with the sane. The things that you see in this hospital in an exaggerated form, you observe in milder degrees outside. It is merely called insanity here and sanity there." He had a sane respect for the insane.

I have never known a man with better judgment, wisdom, and common sense. People came to him for advice on matters unrelated to his work in the hospital. Widows would consult him often how best to invest their money. Others consulted him about domestic difficulties. Young people went to him for guidance in their love-affairs. To one young man, who was recovering from a severe illness and who, in the presence of my father, expressed critical and bitter thoughts about religion, he said:

"I should advise you not to put too much reliance on your present ideas. When you have improved physically, you will be in a better position to think about all these matters and I would advise you not to come to too definite a conclusion until then."

For a considerable time he was an elder in a church at Charlottetown and did a good deal of sick visitation. I have been told many times that his visits in his church district were awaited with eagerness by the sick and their families.

My father had a strong faith in God and believed that religion can minister definitely to the alleviation of mental illness. On all occasions, when a chaplain was not available, he conducted the religious service in the chapel and preached a brief sermon to the patients and the staff. The patients, particularly, looked forward to his appearance in the pulpit because he understood their needs and he talked neither over their heads nor in tones of condescension. Frequently visiting preachers would "talk down" to the patients.

I recall on one occasion that he preached to a crowded chapel on the subject of the peace of Christ. His sermon was based on the words, "Peace I leave with you, my peace I give unto you: not as the world giveth, give I unto you. Let not your heart be troubled, neither let it be afraid." He told his hearers that the peace of Christ takes fear out of our lives, frees us from restlessness and strain, giving to us quietness and serenity of spirit. As he continued his sermon, a great stillness came over the chapel. The murmur of voices, which had been quite audible at the commencement of the service, died away. The shuffling of restless feet was stilled and even twitching bodies became quieter as the eyes of almost all of the patients were fixed intently on his face.

That experience was a revelation to me of the ministry that the Christian faith can exercise in disoriented minds.

My father often said that when a man is mentally deranged, it does not necessarily mean that he is immune to a spiritual ministry. He recognized, of course, that there are types of mental illness which would make it highly inadvisable to leave a man with a copy of the Bible in his hands or to seek to present to the patient religious ideas. He believed, however, that it would be a forward step if, in every hospital for the insane, there were carefully selected and well-trained chaplains. He often said that immunity to one kind of psychotherapy does not make a patient impervious to spiritual help.

In Falconwood Hospital no provision was made for a regular spiritual ministry to the patients. Indeed, the services in the chapel Sunday by Sunday were dependent upon the convenience and good will of visiting pastors. In many cases the only religious consolation given Protestant patients in the institution was afforded through my father's ministrations. Day by day he was accustomed to visit one man, in particular, who was very ill—a man who had been, at one time, a prominent leader in a Protestant church. He sat beside the bed of this man and read to him familiar passages, such as the twenty-third Psalm, and then offered a brief prayer. He told me that he had done this again and again without receiving the slightest indication from the sick man that he had any understanding or appreciation of what was going on. Then, one day, a message was sent to his hospital apartment to notify my father that this man was dying. He hurried up to the ward and into his bedroom. Going up to the bedside, he took the man by the hand and spoke to him, but he made no response. The weakness of his pulse revealed that he was slipping away. As my father stood beside the bed, suddenly the man released his hand from my father's grasp and caught him by the trousers at the knee and commenced to pull down and down. For a moment he could not understand what the patient meant, but, as the sick man persisted, suddenly it dawned on my father that he wished him to kneel in prayer. He did so, asking God to grant to this soul an abundant entrance into His Everlasting King-dom.

My father told me later that, as he rose from his knees and looked at the man's face, he saw understanding, recognition, and a great peace reflected there, and in that moment the patient passed away.

"Religion has power," my father told me, "that reaches past all the barriers erected by mental disease and ministers to the soul of man in his extremity. Sometimes I believe it is under-estimated by physicians. I hope the time will come when it will be one of the extensively used forms of psychotherapy."

Within a week of this happening, my father had passed away. To the very end he continued to ask about patients who were seriously ill.

During the service of my father's funeral, an incident oc-curred which will not soon be forgotten by those who wit-nessed it. At their own request some sixty or seventy patients had been brought into town to attend the service. They sat at the rear of the church and listened, with rapt attention, to the whole service. When the benediction had been pronounced the congregation moved forward, in single file, to look, for the last time, upon the face of the one whom they had known and loved. Last of all came the attendants and patients. As the long line of inmates from the institution filed past, one by one they reached out and touched my father's hands as they lay folded on his breast—hands which they had so often touched in the wards of the hospital. It was their way of saying "fare-well" to one whose hands had so long and so tirelessly min-istered to their well-being.

When I went to the general hospital on the day following the funeral service to secure a few personal effects belonging to my father, I found among them a little vest-pocket diary. The last entry had been made just before he left for the oper-ating-room. It concluded with these words,

"I will fear no evil: for thou art with me."[1]

[1] Psalm XXIII:4.

I was not surprised to find this entry in his diary, for he had approached the end with perfect serenity, his face reflecting "the peace which passeth all understanding." He, whose ceaseless ministrations had driven fear from many a troubled heart, was not bereft of consolation in his hour of need.

II. *An Apprenticeship to the Ministry*

"Let no man despise thy youth; but be thou an example of the believers, in word, in conversation, in charity, in spirit, in faith, in purity."

—I TIMOTHY IV:12

". . . Watch thou in all things, . . . make full proof of thy ministry."

—II TIMOTHY IV:5

TWENTY-FIVE years ago a mental hospital was not regarded as an orthodox place for an apprenticeship to the ministry. In more recent years, however, students at theological seminaries have put in an interneship of from three to six months in mental and general hospitals as a part of their training for the ministry, in an endeavour to acquaint themselves with the problems of human life which, afterwards in one form or another, they will meet in their parishes.

I was but seventeen years of age when I became an attendant or male nurse in the mental hospital of which my father was supervisor. In this institution I was in hourly contact with intensities of abnormal emotions and behaviour which, despite their abnormality, did not blot out activities of the spirit. I saw patients whose minds were distressed by delusions about religion as well as on other subjects, but I saw many more, in the wards of the hospital, who had normal contacts with God.

At that time the special services of an attendant were required for a patient who had proved a source of trouble to the officers of the hospital. He was a brilliant lawyer who had been convicted of embezzlement. During his trial he had been examined by psychiatrists who pronounced him a paranoiac. After he had been committed, by the court, to Falconwood Hospital, his restless, active mind brought him into conflict with the officers and attendants of the institution. He quarrelled with every man who was put in charge of him. Physically the care of this patient was not onerous, as he never became violent. On occasion, however, he would fly into a rage and become abusive.

It occurred to my father that if I were given charge of this patient and requested him to assist me in my studies for college entrance, it would take up his time and thought and relieve his mind of many of the suspicions which he entertained against the officers of the institution, as well as the people outside it, who he believed were plotting against him. It would also relieve him of the feeling that he was a prisoner if he became instructor to me, an attendant in the institution.

I shall always have a vivid recollection of the day when my father led me to Ward Three, which was already familiar to me, and introduced me to Mr. Broadlawn, my special charge.

In the midst of a clump of white birches growing on the bank of a beautiful river, which flowed close by the institution, my patient and I erected a rough shelter and in it spent many hours together over my books. From this man, who was definitely insane, I had my first lessons in geometry, algebra, and Greek, which subjects I had not reached at the time of leaving school. He was a brilliant scholar and a careful teacher. For a period of two and a half years all my preparation for college was made under his direction. He took great interest in my work and became much more coöperative, not only with me but also with the officers of the institution as well.

While he was teaching me modern history at the time of the Agadir Affair in French Morocco in 1911, he made an emphatic prediction that within three to five years Germany would precipitate a general war in Europe.

Periodically I had to take over general duties on the wards and at such times another attendant was placed in charge of my patient. During these periods when I was away from him, he often chafed at my absence because some of the relieving attendants used to ask him to read to them from novels that were far below his level of literary interest. Even on these occasions I used to go down in the evenings to his room, which was off another ward, and have him check over the studies I had completed during the day.

For two years I attended the lectures which were given to the nurses, twice a week, by the medical superintendent.

As we worked together in the shelter we had built by the river, Mr. Broadlawn talked to me of his ideas of God. He seemed especially interested in the fact that already I had some thoughts of the ministry as a profession. Very seldom did he speak of the offences of which he had been convicted, but on one or two occasions he revealed thoughts that were apparently oftentimes in his mind.

He said to me, "You see, I have some debts to pay, an obligation to society and to God. I feel that these debts are going to be very difficult for me to discharge. I have been in this institution now for four years and there is little prospect of my being released any time soon, for the tide of public opinion is running strong against me. You will not be staying here. You are not intended for this kind of a job. There is a bigger world waiting for you. If I can be of any help in training you for college so that the way may be open for you to become a minister, in some measure at least I shall be helping to discharge my debt both to society and to God."

During all the time in which we were together this patient was reading steadily three or four books a week which were borrowed from a near-by public library. Only those who knew him intimately and understood him thoroughly could find the slightest evidence of mental derangement in his words or attitudes. Indeed he was perfectly sane on every subject except those most intimately related to his own personal affairs, and even in this area, his outward reactions were generally normal.

When at times he became intractable, I found that he would immediately respond if I secretly dropped, somewhere in his room, a message requesting a greater measure of coöperation with the hospital staff. I discovered that the message was always more effective if it were written in some type of code, without the key. He would spend hours working out the code and deciphering the message. In matters personal to himself he was always looking for secret messages.

On one occasion for several days Mr. Broadlawn was in a fierce temper. He was angered by a letter which had come to him from a relative who refused to assist him in an appeal for another trial. As he talked about this man he bit clean through the stem of the brier pipe he was smoking. After he had been locked up for the night in his room, I secured an empty talcum-powder can and with a nail wrote on the bottom of it in a simple code

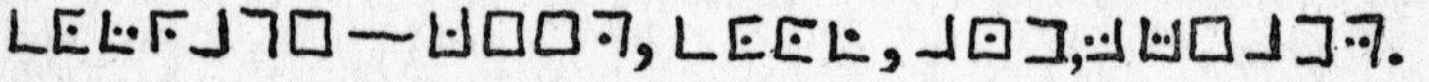

I signed the message with a St. Andrew's cross like the letter X. I chose this symbol because the first name of the patient's father was Andrew.

The same evening I placed this can in a corner of the shelter in which we studied. The next morning when we had settled down to work I saw Mr. Broadlawn furtively slipping the can into his pocket. A few minutes later he excused himself and went for a walk along the shore. When he returned I knew by his happy demeanour that he had translated and read the message:

"Courage—Keep cool and steady."

His bad humour disappeared as if by magic and he was wholly coöperative for weeks afterwards.

Despite the fact that he was convicted of embezzlement, I believe that this man was inherently honest and by the end of five or six months' acquaintance with him I was willing to trust him with anything of value that I possessed.

I learned from Mr. Broadlawn many lessons which are not in text-books. On one occasion when I had completed some translations from the Greek he said to me:

"Did you ever think how difficult it is for a man who is a patient in a mental hospital to prove that he is sane? For instance, there is Mr. Grange on the same ward with me who was examined by a commission the other day. He understood the purpose of their visit and I think he has completely recovered from his illness, but he found it difficult to establish that fact. After they had begun to question him about his thoughts and plans, he became angry and defied them to prove that he had ever done an insane act in his life.

" 'I am just as sane as any one of you,' he said, belligerently. The commission hasn't made its report yet, but I am afraid they will leave him here for a further period. In a mental hospital there is no use in either a sane or an insane man protesting that he is sane. He has to demonstrate the fact in a multitude of ways while he is under observation."

Turning to me, with his pipe firmly gripped in his teeth, he suddenly asked:

"If you were a patient in this hospital and a commission came here to investigate your mental condition, how would you establish your sanity? What would you say to them?"

Without waiting for my answer, he continued:

"After all, who is to determine what people are sane or insane and what is to be the basis of judgment? Thoughts, ideas, and behaviour that might be classified as evidence of insanity in this country in some other nations might be regarded as normal."

"What are you driving at in all this?" I asked him.

"Well," he replied, "if you should go into the ministry, I trust that you will not forget what you have seen in this institution and that you will further develop the understanding you have gained in dealing with those who are mentally ill. If you can learn to combine the knowledge you are gaining here with the power of religion to stabilize human minds, you will blaze trails.

"In my boyhood I went regularly to Sunday school and church. When I entered university and had gone forward to the completion of my course in law, I became very careless in these matters and after my graduation had no contact with the church or religion. I know that I have suffered for this neglect. Among the many things that religion should be able to do for individuals is to keep them steady and serene in mind and spirit.

"Look at that box," he said, indicating a shoe-box that stood in the corner of his room. It was filled to the top with discarded brier pipes and that part of the stem which is held in the teeth had been chewed off each one. "That box," he said, "is evidence that I need something to deliver me from the constant tension I am under."

On one occasion Mr. Broadlawn demonstrated convincingly

how utterly intractable he could become when he was emotionally upset. For a whole month I had been detailed to ward duty and another attendant had been put in charge of my patient. He quarrelled with this attendant and had an explosive interview with the medical superintendent, whom he threatened with a thrashing. That night he went back to his room and refused to leave it. The following day he went on a hunger strike.

When Mr. Broadlawn's voluntary fast had continued for two weeks, the medical superintendent became alarmed. He could have resorted to tube feeding, but this would have been a most disagreeable affair when it involved a man as intelligent as Mr. Broadlawn.

One morning the superintendent stopped to talk with me in my ward.

"I am very much disturbed about your lawyer friend," he said; "he has kept us all guessing now for two weeks and if he persists in refusing food he will die. He was so much more coöperative when you were in charge of him that I have begun to think we made a mistake when we changed that arrangement. You know him so well, do you think you could do anything to induce him to give up this hunger strike? We will have his friends about our ears if he should die."

"I have been watching Mr. Broadlawn very closely for some time now," I said to the physician, "and I think I can persuade him to quit his fast, but it will require a little time and I must have your authority for some of the things that I will have to do."

"Very well," said the superintendent, "I will release you from your duties here if that is necessary, so that you can give your whole time to this matter. If you can get him through this crisis we will give you charge of his case for the rest of the time that you are here."

I realized at once that I was faced with a serious problem. In my contacts with Mr. Broadlawn I had learned to respect his powers of resistance. I knew it would be exceedingly difficult to persuade him to change his mind about the hunger strike. From my observations of his way of sizing up situations I knew that I must do something that would intrigue him —something dramatic and altogether unusual.

That evening as I pondered the matter, I recalled that after I had given Mr. Broadlawn a note which I had dictated but which had been written by a nurse, he had gone to the office and checked over the nurses' report books until he had identified the writer of the note. From that time he became convinced that this nurse was involved in his affairs.

With this fact in mind, I went to the top floor of the female wing where the sewing-room was located. Here I found some pieces of cotton cloth from which the nurses' uniforms had been made. On the reverse side of one of these patches of cloth I wrote "9.05 A.M." with the handle of a pen which I had dipped into an inkwell.

I then composed a letter of instructions to Mr. Broadlawn, again written in code without enclosing the key. In the note I said:

> "Important happenings imminent. You must be ready to act. Terminate fast as quickly as possible under physician's instructions. In 48 hours you will receive another message."

I signed this note with the cross of St. Andrew.

This message I wrapped carefully inside the piece of nurse's uniform. I planned to throw the message through the transom above Mr. Broadlawn's door and needed to make a package of sufficient bulk to attract his attention. Looking around the room for something with which to accomplish this purpose, I noticed a large ball of red yarn on a side table. I wound this yarn around the cloth until it had become a good-sized ball, weighty enough to throw.

I had previously explained to the attendant in Mr. Broadlawn's ward that I was going to throw a message over his transom that night. At nine o'clock, after the patients had all been locked in their rooms, I knocked gently on the ward door, which was opened by the attendant.

I had secured a pillow-sham which was stiffly starched and ran along the ward on tiptoe with short steps, rustling the pillow-sham to make it resemble the sound of a nurse's uniform. On reaching Mr. Broadlawn's door, I threw the ball of red yarn with my message enclosed into his room. It had scarcely bounced on the floor before I heard the patient leap from his bed to seize it, as I was hurrying away, still rustling the pillow-sham.

The next morning when the ward attendant unlocked Mr. Broadlawn's door the patient said to him, very quietly, "I have decided to end my hunger strike this morning."

"Very well," said the attendant, "I will bring you a tray."

For a moment the patient looked embarrassed, and then he said:

"I want you to call the superintendent and get his instructions as to what I should eat."

For twenty-four hours he was given nothing but liquids. The next day he received some solid foods.

About eight o'clock on the evening of the second day I went to the ward directly above Mr. Broadlawn's room, and lowered out the window at the end of a string another message. No sooner had it come opposite Mr. Broadlawn's window than I heard it open and instantly there was a tug on the string for all the world like a hungry trout taking a baited hook. I knew then that the patient had got my message.

In this note, again written in code, I said:

"You are to leave the ward each day at the hour set in the first message. Then you are to go down to the hallway opposite Ward One and look for further instructions on the door of the wardrobe standing in the corner. You are to coöperate wholly with the attendant in whose charge you will now be placed."

I planned at irregular intervals to draw enigmatical symbols on the door of the wardrobe.

Mr. Broadlawn asked me to meet him in the lower hall of the hospital at 9.15. He used to stand at the ward door waiting until it was five minutes past nine and became very indignant if the attendant was not standing there to let him out at that moment, but offered no explanation for this strange behaviour. He never commented to me about having seen the symbols on the wardrobe door.

From the time of this episode until I left the hospital to go to college I was in charge of Mr. Broadlawn, and he was wholly coöperative with me and with the officers of the institution.

An aftermath of this hunger strike completely astonished me. One morning Mr. Broadlawn left a note, in the code which I had used, under the door of the wardrobe on which I had drawn the symbols.

In this letter he expressed his thanks for the suggestions given to him, and then added:

"I am going to be patient in the future because I understand the hint you gave me when I had to unroll all the 'red tape' before reading your instructions."

In that moment I realized that unconsciously "I had builded better than I knew," but I never found out what he thought of the origin of the messages or his interpretation of the symbols I had drawn on the wardrobe.

One of the lessons that I learned from my care of this man was that one may exercise authority over others who are older than he in years, and in certain kinds of experience. I, a boy in my teens, had been given authority over a man who was twice my age, stronger physically than I, and with a far better education.

He said to me once, "I hope you have noticed that although you are only a lad, I do not and never did resent your authority over me. Indeed, I accept it gratefully. I even like it when, in your quiet way, you say firmly, 'It is time now to go back to the institution.'"

With that I recalled something my father had reported to me when I was first put in charge of Mr. Broadlawn. He told me that on numerous occasions Mr. Broadlawn, when out walking, had refused to go back to the institution when the whistle blew for supper and sat down stubbornly in his tracks so that he had to be carried to the hospital on a stretcher. For the most part the attendants were glad to avoid taking care of him because of these "sit-down strikes." I referred to these episodes in light vein as we conversed, and asked him why he had never perpetrated on me such a sit-down strike in all the time I had been with him. He replied simply that no occasion with me had ever aroused his obstinacy.

Then he went on to say: "The first time you came to take charge of me you treated me like a human being. You didn't order me about the moment you arrived. You continued the same cordial attitude you had when you used to walk through the wards with your father on his daily rounds years before you were formally introduced as my mentor. You continued to treat me with as much friendliness after as before our official relationship. That is something which cannot be trained into a man. He either has it or he does not have it. You had it years ago when I first saw you.

"Remember," he continued, "when you take up your life work, that age is not the criterion of authority. Even though you will still be a young man, you will be consulted by people two and three times your age. I trust you will remember that, while physically they may be older than you, spiritually you will be more mature than they and that you will speak to them with the authority of a servant of God."

Under the coaching of this patient I passed the examinations for entrance to college and a few months later began the studies preliminary to university work. I still kept in touch with Mr. Broadlawn, whom I had come to regard as a friend.

On a number of occasions I went out to the institution in the evenings with very difficult mathematical problems that few, if any, of the students could solve. Although Mr. Broadlawn had not studied mathematical formulæ for years, after looking them up in the text-book he would work out these problems with extraordinary ease. He lapped them up as if they were secret codes! One evening when we had just about completed one of these problems, an incident happened that impressed me deeply.

We had been quiet for a little time when I noticed on the window ledge two feet away a mouse. After surveying the room for a moment, he jumped a few inches to the table on which our papers were spread and ran over to where an enamel cup of water was standing by Mr. Broadlawn's elbow. Climbing on to a thick book, he jumped to the rim of the cup and, balancing himself on its edge, he began to drink the water, periodically lifting his head and glancing round the room. After he had taken several drinks, I said to Mr. Broadlawn, "For goodness' sake, look at that mouse drinking out of your cup."

I felt sure he had noticed the mouse before I had said this and he seemed for the moment to have forgotten my presence until my comment roused him. I had interrupted a quiet smile on his face and I felt I was an interloper who had stumbled upon a tryst between two who had formed a lasting friendship. The patient looked at the mouse for a moment and then tapped him gently on the back with his lead pencil, saying, "Get away from my drink, you little rascal." Forthwith, the mouse jumped from the cup and book to the table, not at all frightened, and retraced his way, over our papers on the table, back to the window ledge from which he had come, and disappeared from sight.

I was too surprised at witnessing this little drama to speak. Mr. Broadlawn turned to me with a sad smile and said, "We who are deemed dangerous to society are put behind barred windows and bolted doors, but we are sometimes comforted by the fact that in nature's great family God has provided some creatures who are not afraid of us and who trust themselves to us."

I said nothing for a moment, and noting my silence he said:
"That mouse is my friend and I am his. He trusts me. Did you ever think of the part that trust plays in human life? Whether it be in friendship or family relationships, when trust goes everything else worth while goes with it. Perhaps you

might be interested to know why I helped you with your studies when you were an attendant here. I liked you because you trusted me. I noticed that you didn't watch me with suspicion when I walked a little distance from you into the woods. Even when you went out with me at first and I happened to walk behind you as you were writing at the table, you never betrayed the slightest nervousness and I knew you were not afraid of me. You will never know just how much that did for me."

Before I had entered the university, the Great War broke out. I was continuing my studies in arts at Halifax and residing at Pine Hill Residential Hall. One evening early in the spring I heard my name called out in the lower corridors and one of the students shouted that a man was waiting below to see me. I said:

"Send him up to my room."

There was a knock at the door and to my utter amazement, in stepped Mr. Broadlawn.

I greeted him cordially and said, "How in the world did you get here?"

He replied, "Frankly, I made a key for the ward door and let myself out at night. I have taken every possible precaution so that blame could not be placed on any officer or attendant in the institution. I think that the authorities will be glad to be rid of me and, if I can get quietly away, there will be very little fuss about it. I want to go overseas in the Canadian army. At present I am working downtown for a lawyer and I am just getting enough to pay for my board and lodging. I am now known by another name."

We spent several evenings together and I noticed that although now he had real reason for closing the door and transom furtively on his entrance, it was not he, but I who took these precautions. One day I heard the rumour that some one had telegraphed to the hospital at Charlottetown that Mr. Broadlawn had been seen on the streets of Halifax and that two attendants were to be sent to bring him back. Also I heard, confidentially, that the authorities at the hospital, though they had not legally discharged Mr. Broadlawn, nonetheless regarded him so far convalesced as to be harmless to himself and society and they would not be displeased if he made good his escape and went, as he had long planned, with the Canadian army overseas.

The evenings I spent with him convinced me of his remarkable improvement. The suspicions which had been evident to the staff of the hospital had now disappeared. I felt convinced that he would be a good risk as a soldier. He so wanted to reinstate himself and pay his debt! Accordingly, I facilitated arrangements for his enlistment in the Canadian army and his transfer to an Ontario unit under his assumed name. We both thought it advisable for us not to correspond in case his identity might be discovered.

It was very difficult for me to say good-bye to him when I saw him off on the train for Ontario, where he would take his training for overseas. He turned to me and said:

"Thank you for what you have done for me. I feel that if I come back from the war everything will be different and if I don't come back my debt to society will all be wiped out."

That spring I enlisted in the Canadian artillery, and in September our unit embarked upon a troopship which with five others under the convoy of a British cruiser sailed from Halifax. When we were in midocean as I walked the deck of our ship, suddenly I came face to face with my friend, Mr. Broadlawn, now a sergeant in the infantry.

We had many intimate conversations on shipboard. He told me he had qualified for a commission but thought it better not to accept it. Once again he suggested that we should not correspond with each other.

About ten months later, while at the front line in France, I received a letter from my father with the distressing news that Sergeant Broadlawn had been killed in action. I knew that I had lost a very dear friend and benefactor. Instantly there came to my mind the last words he had spoken to me in Halifax:

"If I don't come back, it will all be wiped out. . . ."

During the years I spent in training at the mental hospital, I learned much from my father. He taught me that a man without medical-school training could yet minister to the mentally afflicted. From my earliest years he made me realize that mental illness is not a disgraceful sickness any more than typhoid fever or any other disease. Part of my experience, continuous from early boyhood, was my own conviction that the mentally afflicted were human beings after all, and that in most cases they did respond to sympathetic understanding, friendliness, and trust, and did get from religion both consolation and strength.

In the closing year of my training in the mental hospital I experienced a dramatic illustration of this conviction. Just before leaving for a vacation of thirteen days I learned that a special night watchman was needed on one of the wards. If I should take over that duty, it would give me a day's extension to my holidays. Accordingly, I volunteered my services.

The patient was a young man about thirty years of age whom I had known before he came to the institution. Everyone in the community in which he lived was ready to vouch for his integrity of character. He was active in church work. Ralph, as he was called, had the reputation of fulfilling every promise that he made. He was violent when brought to the hospital.

One morning when the attendant in charge of the ward unlocked his door, he found that the patient, with the aid only of his fingers, had torn the steel screen from the window. Its frame had been embedded in the brick, but somehow he tore it all away and made weapons of the steel bars that framed the screen. He had ripped the wainscoting off the wall, leaving only the plaster and brick. His room was piled up with two or three feet of lumber as the attendant entered. Ralph seized one of the steel bars and made a lunge at the attendant. The guard dodged quickly as the bar barely missed his head and bit into the plaster two inches. The patient was put into a straitjacket and it was necessary to keep a strap on his ankles because he had leaped from the bench, smashed panes of glass in the windows and broken knobs off the doors with his elbows.

That evening at nine o'clock I took charge of him. Ralph

had now been fastened by the ward attendant not only in a straitjacket and ankle straps, but also inside a canvas hammock which was laced right up to his throat and several restraining sheets were tied at intervals round the outside of the hammock. He was in such a position that apparently he could move nothing but his head. As the day attendant left he said, angrily:

"That will keep the damn rascal for a while."

I saw that the patient had heard him. So I winked at Ralph and said:

"Do you believe that? I don't. But all the same you and I are going to get along all right tonight."

Ralph said nothing, but I knew that we understood each other. After I had chatted casually with him about his friends, school, and church associations, he began to converse pleasantly. The slightest reference to the institution, however, worked him into a rage.

I explained to him that the following morning I was going on a vacation.

"Ralph," I said, "is it agreed that you are not going to give me any trouble tonight? I believe in you and am sure that you will not disappoint me."

"You can count on me," he said, "but this promise doesn't hold good for some other attendants who were a whole lot rougher with me than they needed to be."

At midnight I went down to the dining-room for dinner. When I returned to relieve the guard who had taken my place, I found that Ralph had been quarrelling with him. He was dreadfully excited and by dint of moving his knees an inch at a time he had gradually obtained sufficient leverage to tear his way clean through the side of the strong canvas hammock. The relieving attendant lost no time in quitting the room as he had had an anxious hour.

I went in to Ralph. He was lying half on the bed and half on the floor. The straitjacket was still intact, but the hammock bound him round the throat and was choking him. I lifted him on to the bed and the change of position eased the pressure on his throat.

Then I said: "Ralph, what is the meaning of all this? I thought you told me you were going to be quiet tonight."

He replied, "I don't like that fellow who was on guard while you were away. He punched me the other day when I had a straitjacket on and I haven't forgotten it. I was trying to get back at him. I'm sorry about it and won't cause you any more trouble."

He was silent for a moment. Then calling me by my first name as he was wont to do, he said:

"I have something to ask you. I can't sleep with this thing on my neck. I know you are friendly to me. Will you unfasten it?"

It was necessary for me to do some quick thinking. After considering the facts that the straitjacket was put on only partly because Ralph had been violent and largely because the attendant feared and disliked him, I said:

"Ralph, if I unfasten that hammock at your neck and put the mattress in the corner of your bedroom, will you make no more trouble the rest of the night, no matter who comes round, and ask God to take care of you tonight, and go to sleep?"

"I promise," said Ralph, solemnly.

"Do you give me your word as a Christian?" I asked.

"I certainly do," he replied.

I unlaced the cord of the hammock and set him free save for the fact that he was still in the straitjacket. I put his mattress on the floor in the corner of the room, smoothed out his pillow, made ready the blankets, and, when he had laid down on the mattress, I covered him over for the night. I overheard him saying, quietly, to himself:

"The Lord is thy keeper. He that keepeth thee will not slumber. . . ."[1]

Within ten minutes he was asleep.

This was about one o'clock in the morning. Slowly the hours of the night rolled by with no sound on the ward save the dull murmur of voices from the dormitories and the laboured breathing of my patient. I was sitting in a large leather chair,

[1] Psalm CXXI.

pondering the happenings of the evening. At nine o'clock when I had taken on the extra duty of night watchman, I had just finished a tour of fifteen hours' daytime duty, having begun work on the ward at 6 A.M. I felt very tired and my head was resting on the back of the easy chair as I sat in the dimly lighted corridor.

I remember nothing more until suddenly I became aware of the impression that something was wrong. I looked swiftly round me and saw that the first rays of daybreak were coming through the windows. Immediately I realized that, wearied by the long tour of duty and overcome by the closeness of the atmosphere in the corridor, I had fallen asleep.

Instantly I glanced into the room where my patient had been lying on the mattress and saw that he was not there. Neither was he in the corridor. I was paralyzed with fear. What excuse could I give for myself? What justification could I offer for having fallen asleep on duty? Where now was this dangerous man who had been placed in my charge? Perhaps he was miles away from the institution. On several occasions he had attempted to escape. The morning before, when he had torn the steel screen from the window, only the bars had kept him a prisoner. Had my judgment, after all, been at fault? Had he duped me?

I rushed down the long corridor that led down to the bathroom, which was left unlocked at night. I had got halfway to the bathroom when I saw my patient coming to meet me. He was still in his straitjacket.

Noting the look of anxiety on my face, he said:

"I am terribly sorry about this. I found I had to go to the bathroom and when I went out to ask your permission I saw that you were asleep. I realized how tired you must have been and, knowing that you are going on your vacation later in the morning, I didn't want to wake you. So I just walked quietly by you and was on my way back, hoping that I would get back to my room without disturbing you."

I knew that he spoke the truth. I had no trouble whatsoever with him, and at six o'clock in the morning turned my charge over to the ward attendant from whom I had received him the night before.

He was astounded to find the patient quietly sleeping on the mattress in the corner of the room and the hammock, wide open and torn, still fastened to the posts of the bed.

"You took a big chance last night," he said, looking into the room. "You must have been as crazy as your patient."

"Think as you like about that," I replied, "but I am convinced that if you put more trust in Ralph he will coöperate with you very much better."

Months later, after I had commenced my college course, Ralph, now completely recovered, gave a dinner party in my honour. To the assembled guests he recounted all the events I have just described and declared that he remembered also every other incident that happened while he was in the hospital. He mentioned my having told him to pray and said that his prayer that night was the turning point from illness to convalescence.

Apprenticeships to the ministry are of many different types and may be had in unexpected places. My experiences in a mental hospital were in a very real sense my apprenticeship to the ministry because, like novices at a trade, I was learning the A B C's of the profession that was later to become my life work.

Samuel McComb, D.D., says that the two essential qualities without which one can never be a true minister are, "fellowship with God and sympathy with man."

Even while I was an attendant in a mental hospital I learned some significant facts about God, but, above all else, I learned sympathy for man. It is true that most of the people with whom I was associated on the hospital wards would be classified as abnormal or insane, but by observing these people I learned to understand the thoughts, motives, and reactions of the so-called normal and sane. The patients under my charge were frequently disoriented for places and people and therefore did things which sane people would not do because of the inhibitions that restrain them.

A physician once said to me that when you see a man drunk, you will learn more of what goes on inside him in five minutes while he is drunk than you will by observing him for a year while he is sober. When a man is drunk his inhibitions are relaxed. If he has been harbouring a grudge or dislike against some one, he gives vent without reserve to these hitherto secret feelings. If he is a vulgar man, his vulgarity will become apparent. If he is quarrelsome, he will want to fight.

In a measure, so is it with the insane. Oftentimes in a mental hospital one sees human nature with the emotions of the patients uninsulated. If he understands the insane, he will understand the sane. If he knows how to secure the coöperation of the insane, he will be able to work harmoniously with the sane. If he knows how to minister to the mental and spiritual needs of the insane, he will be able still more effectively to meet these needs in the sane. If he sees evidence of God's presence on the wards of a mental hospital, with clarified vision he will see Him at work in the homes of his parishioners.

The two illustrations which I have recorded in this chapter epitomize my apprenticeship to the ministry. They demonstrate the therapeutic value for both the mental and the spiritual health of the patient of an attitude of sympathetic understanding, friendliness, and trust on the part of those who deal with him.

This is equally true of people outside mental hospitals and is particularly true of individuals who are regarded by society as inherently dangerous. It must be remembered, however, that it is necessary for one to exercise this confidence appropriately and not indiscriminately. There are mental patients, criminals, and other people who cannot be trusted.

There are times when an attitude of inflexible firmness is necessary in dealing with the insane. This is equally true of people in all walks of life who are never likely to become inmates of a mental hospital.

The writer of the Book of Ecclesiastes[2] says:

[2] III:1-8.

"To every thing there is a season,
and a time to every purpose under the heaven;
A time to be born, and a time to die;
A time to plant, and a time to pluck up that which is
planted;
A time to kill, and a time to heal;
A time to break down, and a time to build up;
A time to weep, and a time to laugh;
A time to mourn, and a time to dance;
A time to cast away stones, and a time to gather stones
together;
A time to embrace, and a time to refrain from em-
bracing;
A time to get, and a time to lose;
A time to keep, and a time to cast away;
A time to rend, and a time to sew;
A time to keep silence, and a time to speak;
A time to love, and a time to hate;
A time of war, and a time of peace."

The author might have added that there is a time to be con-
ciliatory and there is a time to be firm. Indeed, this was probably in his mind when he says: "A time to embrace and a time
to refrain from embracing." St. Paul, who was one of the
gentlest of men, realized that there was a time for rigid discipline. When he saw evidence of the spirit of rebellion in the
Corinthian Church, he dealt with the situation resolutely. In
his first Epistle[3] he said to them:

"What will ye? shall I come unto you with a rod, or in
love, and in the spirit of meekness?"

He knew that there were situations that demanded the rod as
well as those that called for the spirit of gentleness. Here, as
elsewhere, he was following in the footsteps of the Master
whose indignation on occasions burst forth with irresistible
force as when He denounced the Pharisees in a terrible castiga-

[3] I Corinthians IV :21.

tion and on another occasion drove the money-changers from
the temple.

There were times in my experience in the mental hospital
when the intractableness of one or more patients threatened
the safety of the rest of the inmates in the ward as well as my
own. Such occasions called for the immediate exercise of authority and discipline. The slightest evidence of uncertainty or
fear on my part would have spelled disaster.

Similar occasions arise in the experience of everyone who
occupies a position of leadership. There are times when all of
us need to be told what we must do, whether we will or no.

The ability to enforce discipline is an indispensable quality
of leadership. I learned this in my school days some years before I became an attendant in a mental hospital. One day all
the pupils of the school I attended were gathered in the assembly hall. The principal was detained at the moment in his office.
The majority of the teachers in the assembly hall were women.
Suddenly the whole school got out of control. The pupils
started to shout and stamp their feet, paying no attention to
the efforts of the teachers to quiet them. The upper floor of
the building was vibrating to the stamping of hundreds of feet.
The teachers plainly revealed their utter confusion and helplessness. Suddenly those of us who were seated with a clear
view of the stairway observed the principal rushing up the
stairs three steps at a time. He fairly leaped into the centre
of the room and then stood rigidly at attention like a commanding officer on a parade-ground. He roared in a voice of
thunder that sounded even above the clamour of the pupils,
"Silence!" Instantly the stamping and shouting ceased. A
death-like stillness came over the room. We understood that
here was a man whose commands must be obeyed. We respected
him for this. Even though we all enjoyed our momentary rebellion, we were greatly pleased that there was some one in the
school who could command us.

This lesson which I learned in public school and in the mental
hospital stood me in good stead during my army days in
France. In the summer of 1917 our battery suffered heavy

casualties from poison gas. In one section alone of eighty-eight men, sixty had to be given hospital treatment and several died within the first twenty-four hours of the gassing. This loss was made good by recruits sent to us from every Canadian artillery unit in France. As usually happened in such cases, the commanding officers sent to us only gunners of whom they were glad to be rid—generally men who had been convicted of many crimes in military life, for every military unit has its "undesirables."

When I returned to our battery position after having received two weeks' treatment in a hospital a short distance behind the front line, I discovered that discipline had largely broken down. As senior sergeant who was given the rank of acting sergeant major, it was my duty to see that discipline was restored.

The first night after I had returned from the hospital, at three o'clock in the morning I was awakened by a corporal who said that a call for action had come from headquarters. We had been ordered to engage immediately an enemy battery.

"But," said the corporal, "both gun crews are hopelessly drunk. They got into a French wine cellar and have carried the liquor into the cellar where they are billeted. I have had to wake up the few men of our unit who are still with us, although they have just completed their tour of duty."

"Where are these new gun crews?" I asked the corporal.

"You will find most of them drunk," he said. "They are over in another part of the basement. I am afraid we are going to have a lot of trouble with them and I don't know what to do."

Hastily I donned my uniform, inserting my bare feet into my military boots, and started for that part of the cellar where these gun crews were located. The corridor wound in and out for some distance underground and, as I got nearer to the section occupied by these men, I could hear their voices raised in shouts, curses, and ribald songs.

The room into which I stepped was thick with tobacco smoke and reeked with the smell of spilled liquor, stale air, and sweaty men. My entrance was unobserved, as they were busy singing, shouting, quarrelling, drinking in typical carousing fashion. The floor was littered with broken bottles, cigarette butts, and parts of soldiers' equipment. A large packing-case in the centre of the room was covered with bottles of absinthe, rum, wine, and other liquors. The men had not taken the time even to uncork the bottles but had broken them off at the necks and poured the contents into their tin cups.

I realized at once that I was in the midst of a group of men who were capable of almost any act of violence. Advancing quickly to the centre of the room, I shouted, "Room, 'shun!" That military command penetrated even into brains that were addled with liquor and every man sprang to his feet, some of them very unsteady. With my heavy military boots I kicked over the packing-case in the centre of the room and sent the bottles flying in all directions.

"Every man of you here," I said to them, "is guilty of a serious military offence. We are not playing now. We are in the front line and an order has come for us to open fire on a German battery. There is not a man of you sober enough to take your place at the guns. You are drunk on duty. I give you exactly five minutes to get into your beds and if there is a single word from any of you for the rest of the night, you will be court-martialed in the morning. Now get out."

They lost no time in scurrying off to their blankets. We had no trouble with them for the rest of the night.

Immediately after breakfast the next morning, when they were a bit more sober, I called these two gun crews out on parade and reviewed the happenings of the previous night. I explained to them that I could put every one of them under arrest and have them tried by court-martial. Their offence was so serious that it would mean a long stretch of imprisonment and they knew what military imprisonment meant.

"You men know," I said, "that that is exactly what you deserve if you got what was coming to you. This battery up to the present has had a good reputation and I am going to see that you don't ruin it. We must have the fullest coöperation between N.C.O.'s and gunners. I don't want to see you get into serious trouble. This time I am overlooking your offence. If it happens again, it won't be overlooked. You will have to take on an extra period of duty in order to relieve the gunners who had to take your places last night."

When I gave the command: "Dismiss," practically all of the gunners came to me one by one and thanked me for having overlooked their offence of the night before. One of the most hard boiled of the lot said to me:

"Last night we got what was coming to us and I want you to know that we are all with you."

The whole point of this incident which I have described is the necessity on occasion of unbending firmness. This is also true in the relations between teacher and pupil, physician and patient, employer and employé, parent and child, minister and parishioner. There are times when a pastor must be ready to tell his congregation with a like firmness, individually and collectively, members and officers, that the interests of the Kingdom of God take precedence over their personal and sometimes selfish and inconsiderate attitudes and actions. A congregation, in common with pupils in a school, soldiers in an army, children in a home, likes to know that the one who is in a position of authority over it knows how to exercise that authority not only in a spirit of gentleness, but also when the occasion arises in a spirit of firmness. The congregation cannot have confidence in its pastor unless he assumes and exercises the authority which is committed to him.

People who are capable of rebelling against authority are generally capable of accepting and obeying it. As a rule, where there is one intensity of behaviour, we may expect its opposite, either apparent or latent. For instance, even Mr. Broadlawn, who at times was so verbally abusive and intractable, could yet become a willing tutor to one who had authority over him; and Ralph, who was disliked and feared because of his violence, could yet be as gentle as a mother. In both cases they responded coöperatively to, and their convalescence began with, my understanding, friendliness, and trust.

The mental-hospital experience I had was followed by university, army life in France, seminary, and public life, and much that I had acquired in the mental hospital I carried over into harmonious relations with my comrades in everyday activities. The insane had been on my horizon from my earliest years and yet they seemed to me as tractable as many of the men and women I have worked with in the university, the army, church, and society.

Earlier in this chapter I quoted the words of Mr. Broadlawn:

> "Whether it be in friendship or family relationships, when trust disappears, everything else worth while goes with it."

He might have added that this is true whether the relationships be that of an insane man and his attendant, a patient and his physician, a pupil and his teacher, a child and his parent, a soldier and his officer, an employé and his employer, or a parishioner and his minister. All of these, each towards the other, in order to carry on happily and constructively, must have his feeling of confidence and trust intact and working in both directions.

This holds good also in our relationship with God. Each individual has basically a need of feeling trust in God and, reciprocally, a feeling of being trusted by God.

This coöperative relationship, which is of the utmost importance in all the spheres of human activity to which I have referred, in the parish is absolutely indispensable. A happy and profitable relationship between pastor and people can be built on no other foundation than mutual understanding, friendliness, and trust between each other and between them all and God.

III. *The Cure of Souls*

I charge thee before God, and the Lord Jesus Christ . . . that thou observe these things without preferring one before another, doing nothing by partiality.

—I TIMOTHY V:21

". . . They that be whole need not a physician, but they that are sick."

—ST. MATTHEW IX:12

". . . When he saw the multitudes, he was moved with compassion on them, because they fainted, and were scattered abroad, as sheep having no shepherd."

—ST. MATTHEW IX:36

". . . He knew all men, and needed not that any should testify of man: for he knew what was in man."

—ST. JOHN II:24, 25

". . . As many as received him, to them gave he power to become the sons of God."

—ST. JOHN I:12.

". . . He said to the woman, Thy faith hath saved thee; go in peace."

—ST. LUKE VII:50

THE primary significance of the cure of souls is the *cura*, or charge, in which Christian ministers accept responsibility under God for the guardianship of the souls entrusted to them.

For the modern-day minister, located in one of our large cosmopolitan cities, the problem of the pastoral leadership of his people is a tremendously complicated one. For instance, he has difficulty in finding his parishioners at home because of the multitude of social, intellectual, and æsthetic pursuits in which people are engaged today. They are spending an ever-diminishing amount of time within the home. If at home they may be entertaining guests at bridge and the minister has difficulty in making them all glad he came. And even if no outsiders are present, he soon discovers that the atmosphere of the modern living-room is not conducive to an intimate conversation which is spiritually helpful.

Many ministers waste their time and energy in making calls without seeing their parishioners. As a result, some call only on those to whom they have phoned to make a definite appointment. Others conserve their time and energy even more by requesting their parishioners to come to the study in the church. This arrangement is usually found to be more satisfactory both to the ministers and to their parishioners.

Any minister who undertakes to meet his people on more than a pleasant social basis will soon learn that their conversation will shortly reveal his parishioners' inner needs. He will find himself coming to close grips with human life. A New York surgeon said to me recently,

> "Tens of thousands of people visit clinics of hospitals and offices of physicians in this city every day, seeking a remedy for physical ills. There are as many sick souls in

51

the city who do not come to us medical men, for we don't give them what they need. You clergymen should be constantly at work ministering to them, even to those whose bodies we treat mechanically."

The suggestion of the surgeon that we ministers have an office to fulfil even with relation to sick bodies is emphasized also by Hawthorne in *The Scarlet Letter*:

> "A bodily disease which we look upon as whole and entire within itself may, after all, be but a symptom of some ailment in the spiritual part."

The reverse of this is also true for, as Lucretius says:

> For when the body's sick and ill at ease
> The mind doth often share in the disease.

It would appear, therefore, that there is a vast area to which our ministry ought to be directed and in which, up to the present, we have attempted little.

The pressure of clamant human needs has driven a great many ministers to the study of psychology and psychiatry, but, if the interest on the part of Christian ministers in these new sciences will result only in transforming pastors into fourth-rate psychiatrists, then we shall be guilty of making nuisances of ourselves and of doing ineffectually what scientifically trained men can do far better. We should always remember and never dare to forget that we are ambassadors of Christ entrusted with a ministry to the spirit and indirectly to the mind and body—a ministry which, therefore, necessarily goes beyond the practice of the psychiatrist or the physician. And since this is true, we should endeavour to keep abreast of the constantly expanding knowledge of the human mind and its workings, so that we may carry on this ministry with greater efficiency and less expenditure of time and energy.

One occasionally meets clergymen who are quite contemptuous of psychiatry. But that is not an unfamiliar phenomenon. There are ministers who are equally contemptuous of Biblical criticism, and who declare with scorn that it has nothing to add to the effectiveness of the minister's message. In both cases one cannot fail to note that the extent of the preacher's appreciation is a directly proportionate measure of his knowledge of the issues involved.

Some ministers, in this matter of personal relationships, are born psychologists but even they have something to learn from the experts in this field. I recall a conversation which I had a year or two ago with one of the most skilful deep-sea fishermen I have ever known. There was very little about the habits of the fish which he did not understand. I was impressed, however, as he told me of a lecture to which he had listened, delivered by a professor of marine biology:

> "Well," said the fisherman, "I've always been a practical man and have had great contempt for talk, especially on this subject of fishin'. That's been the business of me family for generations. But, on the night on which I listened to that professor fellow talk, he told us the reason why we do what we do. Now I'm a better fisherman and I can answer questions, too, as well as catch fish, for I'm usin' me head as well as me arms and legs."

So likewise the minister who values his time and desires to conserve his mental and spiritual resources will inform himself of the teaching of these sciences that deal with the human mind.

Whenever the subject of personal interviewing is mentioned in the presence of ministers, some one is almost sure to say, "I should rejoice in this type of work, but I am not fitted for it. Nobody ever comes to me with their problems." The real tragedy is that all ministers have the opportunity to deal faithfully with individual lives in their congregation, but, unfortunately, many of us are not aware of it. Ask the minister, who is doubtful about his own effectiveness in this work: "Who visited your study yesterday and the day before?" He will reply: "Several people came in, but they did not come to talk about religion. They came to confer with me on other matters."

Here is a typical illustration of what may happen to any minister who is alert to human need.

I looked at the card which a secretary had just laid on my desk. The name read, Mr. Eric Randson. The time had come for my first interview that morning. I knew that the man whose name had been given to me was waiting in the consulting-room adjoining my study.

As I entered this room a young man about twenty-one years of age rose to greet me. He was tall, dark, and well dressed, with an alert expression.

"I'm sorry," he said, "but I fear that I have come to you under false colours. I am a reporter. I haven't come for help on a personal problem. Instead I wish to interview you for my paper."

The young man explained that he had already interviewed four other ministers of the larger churches in Manhattan. He asked me a series of questions about my work, the consulting-room, and the types of persons who came to me for spiritual help. Having written down my answers and his general impressions during the interview, he folded up his notebook, thanked me, and rose to take his coat and hat.

I said, "Just a moment, please. Are you in a great hurry?"

He looked at me a little surprised and replied, "Why, no, but I don't want to take up your time."

"Do you like reporting?" I asked him.

"Yes," he said, "I'm never happier than when I am on the job."

"Then I take it that you *are* happy," I responded, "but are you really happy within?"

For a moment he lowered his head and then replied: "I've interviewed many men and women before this, and lots of ministers, but nobody ever asked me how things go inside me. I've never had any one interested in me in all my life. May I talk to you and tell you what's been troubling me?"

Forthwith he launched into a story that pained him much to tell. In that consulting-room this young man found God and discovered, also, the answer to a problem which he had believed to be beyond solution.

In my interview file there is a letter from Mr. Randson. In

it he says, "My visit to your study marked à new beginning in my life. The victory has been complete and I have won it on the old battleground where before I had always met defeat. Now I know what Paul meant when he said, 'If any man be in Christ, he is a new creature.' "

When a minister conducts an interview with a stranger, or even with some one he has known a long time in a social way but never before in the privacy of a study, several principles should be borne in mind.

First. Very few people, whether parishioners or strangers, who come in to talk to the minister, state frankly and clearly at the outset the real purpose of the visit.

A visitor, beginning with a narrative of trouble, may go on to ask help for others than himself or to protest against what others are doing, to ask advice on some problem not directly related to religion, and lastly, though by no means infrequently, to obtain spiritual help. Sometimes during a whole initial interview he will not tell anything that is of vital importance to the solution of his problem. He comes really to form his estimate of the minister before he tells his story, to decide whether this clergyman is the one who should hear it.

A psychiatrist, practising in New York, told me one day:

"A patient coming for the first time to consult me fills up the entire first hour with data that, important and true as they are, are not vital to the problem. He has to assure himself not by asking directly, but by seeing me, that I understand his kind of a case, that I am not going to disapprove of his behaviour, whether normal or abnormal, and that I will keep his communications confidential."

So is it with the minister in his study. For instance, a young man, twenty-one years of age, came to me. The question he proposed was this: should he undertake a course in Arts or should he take a course in business-training? This was the subject of his discourse during the first hour. I discovered a little later, however, that the real question which he wished answered was whether or not he should *take his own life*. I am quite sure that, when he came to me, he did not intend to disclose the major problem that was troubling him. But deep down in his subconscious mind there was the hope that somehow the minister might be able to help him with this underlying problem, even if he should talk only about the one that was on the surface.

Sometimes it will require many interviews to get at the root of the trouble, but we must be prepared to consecrate our time to this all-important work. The tragic fact is that thousands of people go in and out of ministers' studies all over this land, without having the deep and unspoken needs of their lives ministered to. It is a safe presumption that all the men and women who come to us are in need of spiritual inspiration and help.

Second. Listen patiently to the parishioner who has come to talk with you.

Do not interrupt his story. Silence is golden, especially when some one is unloading his heart to you. Here again we ministers can learn from the psychiatrists. They sometimes listen to their patients by the hour, the only interruption being an occasional question or a mere gesture by the doctor.

It is at this point that most ministers fail in interviewing. They are over-anxious to give advice to people. They want to preach to them, to tell them about God and prayer. There will be a time, of course, for these important considerations, but they should not be intruded before the whole story has been told or before the enquirer is ready to accept help. The first rule for the successful conduct of an interview is—listen. The second is—listen. The third is—listen. Always be on the alert to catch word or phrase that may be a clue to the hidden problem. Try to see and understand the personality behind the explanations and evasions to which you are listening.

Oliver Wendell Holmes in *Elsie Venner* says:

> "The doctor knew the difference between what men say and what they mean, as well as most people. When he was listening to common talk, he was in the habit of looking over his spectacles; if he lifted his head so as to look

through them at the person talking, he was busier with that person's thoughts than with his words."

The minister, too, must learn to see, behind the parishioner's words, his underlying thoughts and motives.

Oftentimes the most urgent need of those who come to us is to find a sympathetic listener. When the surcharged heart has emptied itself of a heavy burden, a long step has already been taken towards complete deliverance and healing.

Nathaniel Hawthorne, in *The Scarlet Letter*, makes the clergyman Dimmesdale say to the physician:

> "Many, many a poor soul hath given its confidence to me, not only on the death-bed, but while strong in life, and fair in reputation. And ever, after such an outpouring, oh what a relief have I witnessed in those sinful brethren! even as in one who at last draws free air after long stifling with his own polluted breath. How can it be otherwise?"

It must be remembered, of course, that the relief which comes from confession is not necessarily release from sin. The minister's main contribution will be made following the confession rather than in eliciting it. The minister must be able to show to the penitent how the acceptance of God's forgiveness and the honest resolve to lead a new life will produce a complete transformation of character.

Dr. C. G. Jung of Switzerland in his book, *Modern Man in Search of a Soul,* states his conviction that the Protestant minister of today stands, at this point, on the verge of a vast horizon of effective service, but seems not to have noticed it.

Third. Do not accept a parishioner's diagnosis of his own problem. Ministers will do well at this point to follow the example of physicians. When a patient comes into the office of a medical man and announces that he is suffering from arteriosclerosis, the doctor does not say: "Now that's too bad. I will make out a prescription for you." He listens to what the patient has to say and then proceeds to make a careful examination and diagnosis of his condition. The pastor in the conduct of his interviews cannot afford to be less discerning.

There was a time when the minister accepted without question the diagnosis which the parishioner made of his own spiritual condition. Then he would conclude a brief interview in which he had done most of the talking by saying, "Go home and read your Bible," or "Pray about this thing," or "Buy such and such a book and read it and come back in three weeks and tell me what you think of it." Fortunately, the number of pastors who apply this hit or miss method is constantly decreasing.

Centuries before Christ, Thales, the philosopher, was asked, "What is most difficult?" and he replied, "To know thyself." Then the questioner asked, "And what is easy?" Thales answered, "To advise another." The second answer might require some revision because it is not easy to give the wisest and the best advice to others. It is easy, however, for us to see their faults and failings.

Psychologists have used the word "rationalization." When people comfort themselves with a false explanation of their attitudes and actions, it is said that they are rationalizing. This is an experience that is true of us all. Generally we put the most favourable possible interpretation upon what we ourselves do and think and say. Consciously and unconsciously we screen the real explanation of our behaviour. We say that it is the other person who is at fault, when the true remedy lies in the difficult adjustment that we ourselves must make within our selves. As Seneca says:

"You must discover yourself in the wrong before you can reform yourself."

Everyone who is accustomed to dealing with individuals has discovered that the average human being possesses an almost infinite capacity for self-deception.

There is simply no limit to the way in which people fool themselves. For instance, a young professional man came to see me. He said that he was an official in a Protestant church and that he taught a large Bible class.

"I'm not the problem," he said, "though it is in my home. Things have reached a crisis there. Neither my wife nor I have actually applied for a divorce, but we are thinking, at the present time, of securing a separation."

"What is the trouble in your home?" I asked him.

"The trouble is with my wife," he said. "We have been married for eight years and have two children. During the first few years of our married life my wife was very careful about the home and was scrupulously neat in her personal attire. She had real abilities. She used to sing well and was a good pianist. The last few years, however, she has become careless about everything—about the home, about her dress, about the children. She never practises her music now and has stopped singing altogether. Things have gone to pieces generally round the house and I am sick of the whole business."

"Well, what would you say is the trouble with your wife?" I asked him.

He said: "I can describe it in three words: lack of discipline. That is what's the matter. She is undisciplined about everything and I don't intend to put up with it any longer."

"You seem to have an analytical mind," I said to him, "and you have made a remarkably good job of dissecting your wife's character. In fifteen minutes you have told me a great many of her faults. Is her personality stronger than yours?" I asked.

"No," he responded. "Why do you ask?"

"Well, if you are the stronger personality, would you mind taking some time now to tell me a few of the worst things about yourself?"

He balked at that and said,

"But I didn't come here to talk about myself."

"That may be true," I said. "Nevertheless, since you say you are the stronger personality, if I am to help you with your problem you must let me see the complete picture of your home life."

"Well," he said, "I have got a bad temper."

"That's a good beginning," I replied, encouragingly. "Tell me some more. How does this temper manifest itself in your home?"

He gave me some details and then added:

"I guess I'm very selfish, too. I like everything in the home to centre round myself. I'm not very considerate, I suppose, of my wife and children."

He continued to recount his own failings until it was quite evident that his indignation at his wife's lack of discipline was due to the fact that he was partially aware of a similar fault in his own life. He was attacking in her the thing that existed in a larger degree in himself.

"Do you think anything can be done about her problem?" he asked, earnestly, as though only she needed help.

I said, "Yes, I'm sure that something can be done."

At this point I passed over to him a New Testament and requested him to read aloud to me the first six verses of the second chapter of the epistle to the Romans. This is what he read:

> "Therefore thou are inexcusable, O man, whosoever thou art that judgest: for wherein thou judgest another, thou condemnest thyself; for thou that judgest doest the same things.
>
> "But we are sure that the judgment of God is according to truth against them which commit such things.
>
> "And thinkest thou this, O man, that judgest them which do such things, and doest the same, that thou shalt escape the judgment of God?
>
> "Or despisest thou the riches of his goodness and forbearance and long suffering; not knowing that the goodness of God leadeth thee to repentance?
>
> "But after thy hardness and impenitent heart treasurest up unto thyself wrath against the day of wrath and revelation of the righteous judgment of God;
>
> "Who will render to every man according to his deeds."

When he finished reading, he looked up at me with an inquiring expression in his face and said:

"Well, what about it?"—this question from a Bible-class teacher!

I said, "Read aloud once more verses one and three," and he did:

> "Therefore thou art inexcusable, O man, whosoever thou are that judgest: for wherein thou judgest another, thou condemnest thyself; for thou that judgest doest the same things. . . .
>
> "And thinkest thou this, O man, that judgest them which do such things, and doest the same, that thou shalt escape the judgment of God?"

As he was reading these verses for the second time the light of understanding came into his eyes.

"I see what you are driving at and I am sure you're right. My own life lacks discipline; every bit of it—my reading, my office work, my business relations, my prayer life, my home, everything. And I have hated myself for it; and I guess I have been striking at the same thing in my wife. I have been as blind as the Pharisee who said: 'God I thank thee that I am not as other men are.' I think that my eyes are now opened to my own faults and I can do something about this right straight off."

Without waiting another minute he shook hands with me and left.

Six months later I received an enthusiastic letter from this man. In it one sentence is outstanding:

"You will be interested, I'm sure, to know that things are now going along gloriously in our home."

It should hardly be necessary for me to press the moral of this incident. There are thousands of people round us every day who are just as blind as was this man to their own inner needs and the urgent necessity of honesty with themselves, with God and with their fellow-men. How true is the assertion of Dr. Karen Horney[1]:

> "It is far more pleasant to feel a righteous indignation at others than to face a problem of one's own."

[1] *The Neurotic Personality of Our Time.*

The case of this professional man is also but one more instance of the way in which a Christian experience that is continuous and progressive will enable an individual to move forward to a solution of his most perplexing problems.

Fourth. Familiarize yourselves with your parishioners' problems so as to develop insight into their basic needs.

Many varieties of people will come to the minister for help. Some of them will be cranks who have a great "revelation" which they are preparing to announce to the world. Some will be definitely insane. Every pastor ought to be prepared ahead of time for such visitors and be ready to deal with them gently and understandingly and yet without the waste of too much time. Other callers to his study will be neurotics with compulsions and obsessions, and also people suffering from various symptoms of physical ills produced by hysteria. In the main, however, those who seek help of a minister are the people who can definitely be classed as "normal"—parishioners and others who are troubled by personal problems that clamour for attention.

When a set of symptoms are announced to the pastor he must realize that what has been told to him is a mere detail of a more extensive pattern. He should look for these patterns in the cross sections of contemporary existence and be able to distinguish them from the longitudinal sections. The patterns we find in the cross sections are generally the parishioner's relationship to his friends, his associates in business, his social acquaintances, the people whom he meets in his church and to God. The longitudinal sections of a behaviour pattern may be seen in his relationships with his family throughout the whole of his life. If he has had difficulty in adjusting himself to his friends, associates, and so forth, it will generally be found that there has been almost a life-long tension in his home, many quarrels and reconciliations, meetings and partings. Pastors should be on the lookout for these behaviour patterns in the lives of parishioners.

A teacher sought an interview with me at the close of a vesper service.

"I would like you to pray for me," she said, "because I am

terribly lonely and feel that I cannot pray to God for myself. I have no friends now in this city. Your sermon made me feel that my loneliness might be helped."

"How does it come that you have no friends?" I asked her.

She said: "There was a time when I had friends, but I have lost them all. In the last four years they have all become estranged. The final blow fell a few weeks ago when a young woman, with whom I came from England, parted company with me. I haven't got a friend left in the world, I haven't even God any more."

"How do you account for the fact that you lost God and all your friends?" I asked her.

"They have no use for me," she said, "because I have become so bitter with them. I have said and written hateful, cutting things."

"You didn't really want to hurt these friends of yours, did you?" I asked.

"No," she said. "That is the strange part of it. The last thing in the world I wanted to do was to offend or to injure them, but something in me drove me to it. Every time I said these nasty things I was sorry for it the moment they were uttered but I couldn't bring myself to tell them so. It's terribly hard for me to go back and apologize."

Upon my questioning her further she admitted that she had been having trouble with her landlord, with her servant in the home, with her grocer and others. In fact, she had fallen out with a wide variety of people. After she had given me these facts there was a prolonged silence and then I said to her, quietly,

"Tell me now, why do you hate yourself so much?"

She looked up with a surprised expression on her face and answered,

"Who said I hated myself?"

I replied: "I know that you do. Your bitterness to others is hatred of yourself that you have projected on to others and on to God. You are following an unmistakable behaviour pattern.

It is not only manifested in your relationships with your friends, but it reappears in every area of your life."

Without lifting her head she replied:

"I do hate myself but I never realized that I had projected it on to my friends and that this is the true explanation of my bitterness to others."

"Do you want me to know still more about you?" I asked.

"Yes."

"Come, then," I said to her, "tell me about that wretched affair you got into three or four years ago which brought all this to a head."

Momentarily a look of fear came into her eyes and then she steadied herself and said, quietly:

"I might as well make a clean breast of the whole affair. It started four years ago with a married man and continued for three years. Then he died suddenly and my whole world was smashed to bits. I had concealed all this from my most intimate friends and they couldn't imagine what was wrong when I had a nervous breakdown. I realized that I had done wrong and there seemed nothing left for which to live. I can see it all clear now. I have been in torment because of an awakened conscience, but there was nobody to whom I could talk. Something you said in your sermon today made me feel that if I told even a little of this to you it would ease the burden of my heart. I would give anything in the world to be able to get rid of this awful feeling of oppression. It has made me unhappy within and bitter to everybody I have known. I am terribly sorry for the hurt I have done to my friends and would like to have their forgiveness and God's."

I talked to this young woman quietly of the infinite mercy of God and of the forgiveness which He freely offers to every "broken and contrite heart." I read to her the story in St. John's Gospel[2] of the woman taken in adultery, who was brought into the presence of Jesus. The Pharisees who held her a prisoner were ready to stone her to death and quoted the law of Moses

[2] St. John VIII.

in justification of this punishment. Jesus replied to them in effect:

"Very well, stone her, but let the first stone be cast by a man among you who has never sinned." Convicted in their conscience and with averted faces one by one they crept out of the Master's presence. Our Lord, who had been writing on the ground, looked up and, seeing the woman standing alone before Him, asked, "Has no man condemned thee?" And she said, "No man, Lord."

"Neither do I condemn thee, go and sin no more."

I suggested to her that our Lord in pronouncing forgiveness upon the woman in the temple not merely assured her that the mistakes of the past had been blotted out but that power would be given to her to become the woman that God had ever intended her to be.

"God offers that power to you now," I added, "for, as St. John has said, 'As many as received him, to them gave he power to become the sons of God.' "[3]

We knelt together in the vestry of the church, and she asked God to forgive the sins of her past, to take out of her heart the bitterness which had produced so much unhappiness in herself and friends, and to give to her power to adjust her life and to become the woman that He had ever intended her to be.

Rising from her knees, she said:

"I feel as though some intolerable weight that was crushing the very life out of me had been lifted from my heart. I know that things will be different in the future. I am going to write to my friend who came to this country with me and ask for her forgiveness as I have asked God's forgiveness. I feel," she said with a smile, "that I am like Scrooge in Dickens' *Christmas Carol*, I have a lot to make up for, but, with God's help, I know that I shall succeed."

Whenever one finds an individual who has become a fount of bitterness, taunting and criticizing people, saying cruel things that wound the heart of friends, one may be sure that he is dealing with some one who hates himself, who loathes and de-

[3] St. John 1:12.

spises himself, and that the bitterness manifested by such a person is but the projection of his own contempt for himself. The pastor who has trained himself to deal intelligently with people will recognize in them the symptoms of inner need manifested externally by various types of human conduct and will endeavour to minister to these people understandingly and bring to them the healing power of God.

Fifth. No clergyman can adequately minister to the deepest needs in human hearts who has not learned to deal effectually with his own.

A great deal of modern preaching lacks vitality and effectiveness because it does not reach men and women at the plane on which they live. In other words, the preacher is not conversant with their inner aspirations, their failures, their temptations, their weaknesses, their sins.

In a preface to a volume of sermons by the Rev. F. W. Robertson, of Brighton, there occur these words written by an observant layman:

> "Many are miserable in their inmost hearts, who are light-hearted and gay before the world. They feel that no heart understands theirs, or can help them. Now, suppose the preacher goes down into the depths of his own being, and has the courage and fidelity to carry all he finds there, first to God in confession and prayer, and then to his flock as some part of the general experience of Humanity, do you not feel that he must be touching close upon some brother-man's sorrows and wants?"

All this is just as true of personal interviewing as it is of preaching except that, in the case of the interview, the minister must have a still deeper knowledge of the human heart and to possess that knowledge he must, first of all, have learned to know his own.

Matthew Arnold said of Goethe that he was able to lay his finger, with unerring accuracy, upon the real seat of human misery and ill, and say, "Thou ailest here and here." Whether

or not that be true of Goethe, certainly it was true of Jesus
Christ. The Evangelist John says:

> "He knew all men, and needed not that any should testify
> of man: for he knew what was in man."[4]

During an interview with Nicodemus, Jesus laid His finger
unerringly upon this Pharisee's complacency and spiritual pride.
In the case of the young ruler the Master pointed to his pos-
sessions, round which his heart was entwined. In the home of
Zacchæus Jesus revealed to the tax-gatherer his dishonesty, his
greed, and his bitter resentment of the hate of his fellow-
citizens. Sitting by the well of Sychar, He placed His finger
unerringly upon the moral problem in the life of a Samaritan
woman. "He knew what was in man." He possessed the power
of bringing people face to face with their real selves and with
God. And He expects those who are His followers to exercise a
like ministry.

Most psychiatrists believe that before they go far into active
practice with mental patients of any kind they should supplement their intramural medical, general hospital, and mental
hospital training with a psychiatric training of their own minds.
To this end they submit themselves as patients to be examined
and treated by another psychiatrist whom they choose because of
his training, experience, position, or character. They submit the
whole of their lives to his scrutiny and analysis:—their feelings,
emotions, their thoughts, words, and deeds; barring nothing,
baring all.

A psychiatrist believes that until he has found in himself
some degree of each and every kind of tendency and knows how
it behaves, how to start it into action, how to stop it, and how
to regulate it into control, he will be unable to recognize and
treat such symptoms as patients will present him. Or, in other
words, he searches into himself until he is able, when with a
patient, to say silently to himself, "Yes, I, too, have been there
and I know the way to and from such a condition." He works

[4] John 11, 24 and 25.

at himself with his psychiatrist-analyst an hour a day for a year, two years, three years—until he believes that he knows himself. Then he knows others.

Psychiatrists expect more of themselves than they do later of their patients and subject themselves to the greatest possible scrutiny for they must be leaders of those in trouble. No matter how depressing and deflating an experience it is, they undergo it having constantly in mind the future therapy of their patients.

Ministers, on the other hand, graduate from their seminaries and undertake the responsibility of directing the work of a church, without having had much, if any, enquiry into their habits of personal devotion and, in particular, into their own ways of sinning.

I am convinced that one of the reasons why ministers oftentimes fail in their work is because they have so little understanding of themselves. I do not recommend that a minister should be psycho-analysed just for training in the ministry. Indeed, I seriously question the wisdom of such a step. Nor do I recommend, of course, that all knowledge gained by psycho-analysis should be avoided by ministers. I do think that, at whatever cost, in so far as he is able to do so he should carry out the injunction of Solon of Athens: "Know thyself."

One of the ways in which this knowledge may be achieved is for the minister to sit down with a brother minister whom he both loves and trusts and who both loves and trusts him in spite of anything he may have to say, and there, in the presence of God, unveil his own heart. His friend will help him to discover those areas of his life that need to be surrendered to the will and power of God. Herein lies one of the differentiating techniques—a minister, not a psychiatrist, admits God into the problems at hand. If this self-examination is performed earnestly, thoroughly, prayerfully, it will produce marked results in a deeper consecration. It will open the minister's eyes to hidden weaknesses in his own life, of which he was unaware. The Rig Veda, a Hindu Scripture, contains an apt observation on this point:

Men soon the faults of others learn.
A few their virtues, too, find out.
But is there one—I have a doubt,
Who can his own defects discern?

How can a minister detect the hidden resentment buried deep in the life of an enquirer unless, first of all, he has learned to recognize this insidious sin in his own heart?

This same need holds good in the case of fears, jealousies, obsessions of inferiority or superiority, marital problems and tensions, morbid thoughts, undisciplined desires, and the thousand other ills that afflict mankind. The minister who deals superficially with his own weaknesses is bound to deal inadequately with the frailties of others.

If a minister has never known the release and joy that comes from a full confession of sin and the acceptance of God's forgiveness, how can he lead burdened souls into such a cleansing experience?

As a matter of fact, however, confession to God alone is sometimes used as an escape from facing the reality of wrongdoing. Undoubtedly there are many people, especially among earnest and well-instructed Protestants, who, in private prayer to God and in secret confession of sin, gain the full assurance of His forgiveness and the power to lead a new and better life. But there are multitudes of others who will be best helped by having a witness to this transaction between the soul and God.

In my own ministry I have discovered that parishioners will find it much easier to make a clean break with the sins of the past if they have undergone the humiliating experience of permitting me to know the wrongs which they have done. Recently I came upon an enlightening comment upon this point from a most unlooked-for source. Seneca, in one of his epistles, says,

"It is a true saying which I have found in Athenodorus: 'Know that thou art free from all desires when thou hast reached such a point that thou prayest to God for nothing except what thou canst pray for openly.' But how foolish men are now! They whisper the basest of prayers to heaven; but if anyone listens, they are silent at once. That which they are unwilling for men to know, they communicate to God."

The Roman philosopher was keenly aware of the effect which is produced upon ourselves when we know that our inner life is exposed to the view of a fellow-creature.

All our relationships with others, in personal interviews, will demand penetrating insight into human hearts and minds. We must remember, of course, the words of Dwight L. Moody:

"No man can lead others nearer to Christ than he is living himself."

It will avail us little if we can bring to needy lives only a second-hand experience of Christ, if we are compelled to go back to the Acts of the Apostles for evidences of God's power in human lives. We need a contemporary Christian experience. We ministers must reserve a portion of every day for self-examination and communion with God. The unfailing result of this spiritual discipline will be an inner serenity and poise, a quietness and confidence which will enable us to minister effectively to the fevered and disoriented lives that come to us for hope and healing.

Sixth. Every confidence entrusted to us in personal interviews must be kept inviolate.

In the Roman Catholic Church adequate provision has been made on this point. The canon law says:

"The priest who breaks the seal of the confessional remains under ex-communication. This law admits of no exception."

So binding is the confessional vow upon a priest that he will not speak to a penitent, outside of the confessional, upon the subject of matters which he has confessed, unless that individual has first given him permission to do so. Neither by word, nor by sign, will he betray a confidence given to him.

Unfortunately the same thing cannot be said of Protestants. That is especially true, in recent years, of religious movements that have emerged. Sometimes in ordinary conversation and in public addresses confidences are shockingly betrayed. No minister or Protestant layman should reveal in a public meeting, in personal talk, or in any printed form, a confidence entrusted to him by some burdened soul who has come to him for help.

There are, of course, occasions when one person's problem may be identical with that of many others, and the recital of how one individual has found release may be an inestimable blessing to a multitude of people. Whenever this is done, however, scrupulous care must be observed, as it has been observed in this volume, that the identity of the individual concerned can never, by any possibility, be discovered. In some instances, so salutary may be the lessons to be gained from one penitent's experience that his permission may be obtained to use the salient facts of his case in the service of other needy lives.

The necessity of keeping every confidence entrusted to us is especially incumbent upon ministers. Our ordination vow should, in itself, be a guarantee that no trust will ever be betrayed.

In an article recently written in *The Christian Century*, on the subject "Betraying the Confessional," Frances J. Nickels says:

> "Not long ago I was in a city, a stranger. When Sunday came I sought as usual a church where I might worship. The young minister preached a stirring sermon to inspire a sense of responsibility toward the social order. To illustrate his point he told the story of a man he called his 'unnamed friend'—how the friend had come to him in strictest confidence with a problem of great importance in connection with a certain welfare project. He wanted to talk over with him a large gift that he wished to make for its support and which he preferred to be anonymous. As the preacher developed his illustration point by point, I recognized the man he portrayed as one of my friends, a modest, reserved person who would be outraged to have himself

and his benefactions thus discussed, even though he was held up as a shining example. He is the sort of man who would not want even his left hand to know what his right was doing, and here he was being shown off as Exhibit A! The service ended, the minister in friendly fashion waited at the door to greet the congregation. Having introduced myself, and assured that no one else could overhear, I remarked, 'That was a fine tribute you paid to Mr. A.'

"Surprised, he said, laughingly, 'Why, did you recognize him from my description?' 'Indeed, with so vivid a portrayal I do not see how anyone could fail to do so,' I replied. 'How fortunate,' he responded, 'that I said only good of him. It would have been all the same if I had criticized him, wouldn't it? It shows how careful one should be in talking of his friends in public.' I wanted to say, 'I know that if he could have listened in today he would have felt that his confidence had been flagrantly betrayed.' Perhaps I shirked a true responsibility."

Such a breach of confidence is almost unbelievable and altogether without excuse. I am quite sure this case is not at all representative of the Protestant ministry as a whole; that it is in truth a rare exception. Few people would come to us with their confidences if they suspected that the subject-matter of their confessions would promptly be relayed to the public in sermons, in conversations, or through the press.

It is a striking fact that the courts of law in this nation are beginning to recognize that a Protestant minister has the right to keep inviolate the confessions that are entrusted to him.

A case in point occurred during the year 1931 in Minnesota. The Rev. Emil Swenson was commanded by the Hennepin County District Court to reveal, in a suit for divorce, information that had been given to him by a parishioner seeking spiritual counsel. The Rev. Mr. Swenson refused to give testimony. He was found guilty by the presiding magistrate and sentenced to a fine of one hundred dollars or thirty days in gaol. The Supreme Court of Minnesota, however, reversed this ruling and freed the minister. Meanwhile the Minnesota legislature has taken steps to remove any ambiguity in the former law and to make clear the right of all Protestant ministers to refuse to divulge information contained in confessions made to them.

Every medical doctor, on his graduation, takes the Hippocratic oath in which he pledges himself not only to keep inviolate all information that has come to him in the course of his practice, but also to refrain from gossip. The section of the oath which deals with these matters reads as follows:

> "And whatever I see or hear in the course of my profession, as well as outside my profession in my intercourse with men, if it be what should not be published abroad, I will never divulge, holding such things to be holy secrets."

My experience would indicate that this section of the Hippocratic oath is conscientiously observed by physicians in general, though there are always a few doctors, as there are some ministers, who forget their obligations. In both cases, however, these are the exception rather than the rule.

Not even a thorough understanding of modern psychiatry, or faithful attendance at mental case clinics, can ever replace, in the life and work of a minister, an experimental knowledge of what God can do for a man. Oftentimes we shall be called upon to rekindle faith in hearts where its flame has flickered and gone out. We shall need to teach people how to pray, how to read the Bible so that its message may have a definite and personal application to their inner needs, how to enter into a fellowship with God so intimate and real that life shall become an unbroken pilgrimage with Him.

It will not be the task of ministers, as some have recently assumed, to make our religion more psychological. Our responsibility will be fulfilled only as we make our psychology and our psychiatry more religious and employ them effectively in the service of God and of the human soul.

IV. *Why Are You Afraid?*

"Why are ye so fearful? how is it that ye have no faith?"

—St. Mark iv:40

"There is no fear in love; but perfect love casteth out fear: because fear hath torment. He that feareth is not made perfect in love."

—I John iv:18

"Be not afraid of them that kill the body, and after that have no more that they can do."

—St. Luke xii:4

"I sought the Lord, and he heard me, and delivered me from all my fears."

—Psalm xxxiv:4

A young man came to me for help in dealing with the problem of fear. I find that I had jotted down the following facts and impressions after his first visit.

Married for ten years. Three living children—aged two, four, and six.

Age: Thirty-five.

Good personality.

College graduate. Cultured and good conversationalist.

Religion: Protestant. Presbyterian. Regularly attends church, but his previously strong faith in God shaken by unsolved problem of fear.

Employment: Brokerage office.

Social interests: Varied. Skates, plays tennis, attends movies.

Physical health apparently normal.

Emotionally unstable. Reveals, on close acquaintance, definite nervous strain. Sleep broken frequently by terror dreams.

Meeting this man casually, one would have said that he was quite a normal individual. But beneath this seemingly placid exterior was inner turmoil and nervous tension. The strain had already made itself felt in his home. When he returned from the office, tired by a heavy day's work, the laughter and play of his children annoyed him. He was irritable with his wife.

"My trouble," he said, "is with fear. For fifteen years it has made my life miserable. I wake up in the night with the feeling that my heart has ceased to beat and that I am about to die. A cold perspiration breaks over me and I suddenly am aware that my heart is thumping rapidly and violently. Often I tremble at these times. The attacks come upon me sometimes in the midst of a busy day, and I experience a strange sinking sensation. I am constantly obsessed with the fear of sudden death. Everything I see round me suggests this thought."

On questioning this young man, I found that he had been examined by a competent physician, who found nothing organically wrong with his heart. On the advice of this doctor he went to a neurologist. The specialist urged him to forget these obsessions, declaring that they were altogether groundless, as he was in good health. The young man left the doctor's office greatly encouraged. All the helpful results of two visits to the neurologist were completely destroyed, however, by a telegram which the young man received as he was preparing to leave for a third visit to the doctor. The message read,

> "Your appointment for this week is canceled. Dr. K——
> died last night."

It was signed by the doctor's secretary. On enquiry he discovered that the neurologist had dropped dead.

When this young business man came to me, he was on the verge of nervous collapse and had practically decided to resign from the brokerage office at which he worked. As I talked with him on various occasions, I discovered that, when he was about five years old, he had received a serious shock at the time of the sudden death of his grandmother in his home. When he had asked his parents why his grandmother no longer appeared, they told him that she had gone to God. But he was much more impressed when a neighbour boy, nearly twice his age, informed him that his grandmother had been put into a hole in the ground because her heart had stopped beating. Unquestionably this experience, the memory of which had been buried deep in his subconscious mind, had contributed not a little to his distress.

While he admitted that it gave him an immediate sense of relief to know something of the origin of his fears, he said, "I still feel, however, that the threat of sudden death is hanging over me." So persistent was this fear it was obvious that there were other contributing causes. I did not assure him that his fear of sudden death was groundless. On the contrary, I admitted the possibility of it, but suggested that heart failure would not likely be the cause. "No one of us," I said, "when we leave home in the morning to go to our work in this over-crowded city can be sure that he will live to see the end of the day. One has only to glance at the statistics of street accidents, many of them fatal, to realize that we all must face the possibility of sudden death." Then I said to him abruptly, "Why are you afraid of life?"

He looked at me in astonishment and said, "What do you mean?"

I replied, "Most people who fear death are afraid of life."

Then I read to him a paragraph from each of two letters which had come to me in response to a radio broadcast on the subject of "Fear." The first was from South Carolina and dealt with the fear of death:

"I fear death—not what is coming after my spirit leaves my body—my fear is for the hour or days before the breath ceases. I have prayed over it and for a time thought of death as only going to sleep. Then the fear returns."

The second was from Maryland and dealt with the fear of life:

"Lately I have experienced a feeling of fear, which distresses me. I have struggled desperately to overcome it. It is not death that I fear, but life itself and all that goes with it."

To the young man I said, "It may seem to you that these are two distinct problems requiring separate and individual treatment. As a matter of fact, they are basically the same. Fear of death is invariably a reaction from fear of life. Montaigne stresses this fact in one of his essays on philosophy when he says, 'He who should teach men to die would, at the same time, teach them to live.'"

"Tell me now," I said to the young man, "what is there hidden deep within you that makes you afraid of life? What are you most ashamed of?" Soon his story came out in halting sentences. He had been morally defeated. He had never succeeded in achieving self-mastery, and a sense of frustration dominated his life. Always he was haunted by the fear that some of his past misdeeds would be exposed. He made a full confession of his wrong-doings, without any reservation. It was accompanied by the resolve that, with God's help, he would live a new and better life.

I explained to him that the sense of shame and frustration which he had experienced as a result of hidden sin had been driven deep down into his life by constant concealment. The repressed fear of exposure had linked itself with the fear of death which had been implanted in him at the age of five. These inner fears, largely unconscious, were screened by a conscious fear of sudden death. I suggested to him that his grandmother may very well have told him that God was angry with little boys who did wrong and that, even at the age of five, he did not look forward, with any eagerness, to meeting God. Thus a sense of guilt may have existed even before his grandmother's death.

It was only when he had made a complete confession that he was able to see the connexion between the wrong-doing which he had admitted and the conscious fear of sudden death which had served as a blind to his real need.

I read to him, one after another, God's promises of forgiveness:

"I, even I, am he that blotteth out thy transgressions . . . and will not remember thy sins."[1]

"As far as the east is from the west, so far hath he removed our transgressions from us."[2]

"I acknowledged my sin unto thee, and mine iniquity have I not hid. I said, I will confess my transgressions unto the Lord; and thou forgavest the iniquity of my sin."[3]

"Though your sins be as scarlet, they shall be as white

[1] Isaiah XLIII :25.
[2] Psalm CIII :12.
[3] Psalm XXXII :5.

as snow; though they be red like crimson, they shall be as wool."[4]

With great gladness he accepted God's forgiveness and, in a prayer of thanksgiving, poured out his gratitude for the almost unbelievable sense of deliverance that had come to him and the quiet confidence and peace that reigned in his heart.

A letter came to me from this young man a year and a half after our final interview. In it he tells of his complete freedom from the fears that had dogged him day and night for fifteen years.

Fear is unquestionably one of the scourges of mankind. Basil King, in his book, *The Conquest of Fear*,[5] testifies to the wide extent of this malady:

> "Everyone is living or working in fear. The mother is afraid for her children. The father is afraid for his business. The clerk is afraid for his job. The worker is afraid of his boss or his competitor. There is hardly a man who is not afraid that some other man will do him a bad turn. There is hardly a woman who is not afraid that things she craves may be denied her, or that what she loves may be snatched away. . . . I am ready to guess that all the miseries wrought by sin and sickness put together would not equal those we bring on ourselves by the means which perhaps we do least to counteract. We are not sick all the time; we are not sinning all the time; but all the time all of us—or practically all of us—are afraid of someone or something."

Basil King, like a great many writers on the subject of fear, does not distinguish between

(1) Appropriate fear of reality in the world outside the individual.

(2) Inappropriate anxiety arising within the individual him-

[4] Isaiah 1:18.
[5] Doubleday Doran and Company, Inc., publishers, Garden City, New York.

self, not related to outside reality and not based on reality within himself.

The first type of fear is normal and seldom causes a prolonged distress. The second type is abnormal and we should seek to gain deliverance from it. Throughout the whole of his book on *The Conquest of Fear* Basil King fails to distinguish between normal and abnormal fears and is thus liable to beget confusion in the reader's mind.

Probably the best way to attack this problem is to remind ourselves that fear has a constructive as well as a destructive function. Appropriate fear of reality may well be normal and constructive. Inappropriate anxiety is always abnormal and destructive. Few instincts are of greater value than normal fear in preserving life. You can see that clearly if you study animal behaviour. Some creatures are not capable of defending themselves with teeth or claws, but nature has provided them with an equally effective method of defence—flight. And fear provides them with the alertness and mobility necessary to escape their enemies. The instinct of fear is acute in the deer, the antelope, the rabbit, and many other animals. It ensures their self-preservation.

Despite much that has been said to the contrary, normal fear performs a useful function in the lives of children. They should develop a wholesome dread of speeding motor-cars and trains that thunder by. They must early learn the danger of poisons. They should be cautioned against drinking liquids found in bottles, or eating any confections they chance to come upon. They must learn that it is the part of wisdom to avoid contact with infectious diseases. It is perilous to neglect this phase of a child's training.

Dr. Smiley Blanton, in his book, *Child Guidance,*[6] upholds this viewpoint when he says: "There has been in the not very distant past almost a cult built up around the idea that fear is unhealthy from the standpoint of mental health. To fear un-

[6] *Child Guidance,* by Smiley Blanton, B.S., M.D., and Margaret Gray Blanton, The Century Company, New York.

wisely is destructive, but to fear wisely is the best of mental hygiene."

A psychologist, in the course of an address some time ago, told of a family in this country that had only one child. Every possible protection was placed round the infant and definite efforts were made to exclude from the child's mind all realization of fear. It had been brought up to be afraid of nothing. One day the garden gate was left open. In a moment the little one rushed gaily out on to the roadway and was killed by a speeding automobile. Edmund Burke was right when he asserted, "Early and provident fear is the mother of safety."

All this is equally true of adults. Normal fear leads to efficiency. It makes the driver of an automobile more heedful to avoid pedestrians. It makes the pilot of the air liner more alert for the safety of passengers. It makes the druggist more careful as he dispenses a prescription. It gives greater caution to the surgeon each time he lays hold of a scalpel in the operating-room.

Sometimes, however, due to an unhealthy mental condition, the normal fear may be transformed into an abnormal anxiety. In such circumstances, it becomes destructive and leads to inefficiency. In such an eventuality the individuals whom I have named would become incapacitated for their tasks. Then the driver of the motor-car would become a menace. The pilot of the plane would be unequal to his responsibility. The druggist would be telephoning to nurses in sick rooms to send back the medicine which he had prepared, in case he might have made a mistake in compounding it. And the surgeon's hand would tremble so violently as to endanger the life entrusted to his skill. We ought to understand that only normal fears and not abnormal anxieties are beneficial to mankind.

Professor J. A. Hadfield, in his book, *Psychology and Morals*,[7] makes this distinction abundantly clear. He reminds us that the protection of civilized life gives to human beings a much greater capacity for fear than they are able to utilize. The result is that it often operates in abnormal ways. The

[7] Robert M. McBride & Company, publishers, New York.

superfluous and inappropriate fear thus becomes one of the chief foes of man's happiness.

Says Professor Hadfield:

> "We should distinguish fear, anxiety and phobia. *Natural fears* are fears directed to objects really dangerous to life: *anxieties* are fears without an object, and are usually due to fear of a threatening impulse within. They are *unrecognized* fears of ourselves. *Phobias* are fears attached to objects not in themselves dangerous. They are *projected* fears of ourselves. This is true of all phobias— they are all fears of ourselves, fears of some impulse in ourselves, fears of 'unconscious desires.' The greatest fear of civilized man is himself. The difference between a normal fear and an abnormal fear (or phobia) can easily be recognized. The normal fear leads to biological efficiency, whereas the abnormal fear leads to inefficiency."

The type of abnormal fear which concerns a minister most of all is, of course, the inappropriate anxieties that so often destroy the peace of mind and heart of his parishioners. It may manifest itself in fear of death, as in the case of the individual of whom I have written at the beginning of this chapter. Its presence may be revealed in a fear of illness that has no physical justification, in a fear of people, fear of the past, fear of exposure, fear of loneliness, fear of secret sins, fear (abnormal) of God, fear of a mysterious, impeding calamity that eludes description. These are the abnormal fears which the minister, who sees his people in personal interviews, is meeting with every day. They are utterly destructive of mental health and physical well-being. They prevent people from seeing God, from finding anything meaningful in prayer, from enjoying the services of a church, from experiencing the joy of living.

How shall we deal with these destructive anxieties when they become a menace to our happiness and peace? One oftentimes hears people say to a friend who is burdened with anxieties, "Your fears are just imaginary. Snap out of it. Forget about them." The intention of these people may be good, but their advice is definitely bad. The trouble with many people is that they try to forget their fears. They push them down into the subconscious mind, where they forthwith begin to produce all manner of nervous disorders. I am not an alarmist when I say that to follow persistently that foolish method is to set your feet on the road that leads to mental breakdown.

I recall an interview which I had with a woman who was a social leader in an American city. Her friends became perplexed and anxious about her. She began to decline all social engagements. She avoided her former acquaintances. Her only sister, with whom she lived, knew that she was not sleeping at night. She became markedly irritable and began to develop symptoms of heart trouble. Her doctors could find no physical basis for her distress. On occasions she told her sister that she was going mad. Unceasingly she contemplated and threatened suicide. The abnormal fear of insanity was continuous.

When she opened the conversation with me alone in the vestry of a church, she talked about her sister as though she were the one who needed help. It was not until more than an hour had passed that she came to the real problem. Then this woman, who was about fifty-five years of age and unmarried, confessed that thirty-five years before she had given birth to an illegitimate child. She was successful in concealing her secret even from her sister. For some years she had succeeded in bearing up under the strain of the dark secret she had locked within her heart. But always there was the haunting dread of discovery. No human being knew her secret. The attending nurse and doctor were both long since dead. But God knew. She could never escape that fact but had not squared her account with God.

When she had finished her story, I opened my Bible at St. Luke's Gospel[8] and read to her of the visit of Jesus to the home of a Pharisee. No sooner had the Master seated himself at the table than a woman of that city, who had grievously sinned, fell at the feet of Jesus, utterly overcome with contri-

[8] Luke VII:36-50.

tion. Her tears of penitence rained upon the Master's feet and she dried them with the hairs of her head and, kissing his feet, anointed them with ointment she had brought. The Pharisee, who had invited Jesus, was incensed at the woman and, were it not for the Master, would have driven her from his home. She had violated the moral code of that day and, in the eyes of this self-righteous Pharisee, was an outcast. But Jesus rebuked the Pharisee, telling him that this despised woman had received Him with greater courtesy than His rich host. Her devotion had been prompted by her sorrow for sin and by her love for the understanding and compassionate Jesus. Bending over the woman, the Master said: "Thy sins are forgiven. Go in peace."

"Peace," exclaimed the woman who sat before me. "I would give anything in the world for even a few hours of peace. For thirty-five years I have been in torment."

"That is exactly what God is ready to give you now," I said to her. "Not only will He blot out the mistakes and failures of the past, but He will give you power to live a life of serenity and peace. Jesus had faith in the woman who came to Him that day in Simon's house," I said to her, "because He saw within her the woman that God had always intended her to be. He sees that woman in you now. He is not condemning you. He knows far better than I do why you failed in the past, and He offers you now a new beginning and 'the peace of God which passeth all understanding.'" "I am ready now," she said.

We knelt together in the quiet vestry and she thanked God for His forgiveness and the gift of His peace. When she rose from her knees, the nervous tension had already relaxed. After several interviews all symptoms of her trouble disappeared. Today that woman is living a normal and happy life, actively engaged in the work of a large church, with a faith in God greater than she had ever known.

Whether the anxiety that distresses us be due to a moral lapse in the past, dread of illness, or some other cause, we should never try to forget these fears. We should not repress them or bottle them up. A repressed anxiety or fear is like an abscess : the poison should be let out, otherwise it will manifest itself in fresh disorders. "Fretting and worry over the possibility of having a disease as cancer has been known to bring on chronic states of ill health," says Dr. Frederick W. Parsons.

The way in which our Christian faith assists us in conquering fear is clearly revealed in the life of Jesus. One instance in particular is enlightening. It is recorded in the Gospel[9] that the Master, who was physically exhausted after a long day of preaching, suggested to His disciples that they should secure a boat and cross over to the other side of the Sea of Galilee. As they set sail, Jesus laid His head upon the helmsman's pillow in the stern of the boat and, rocked by the gentle motion of the waves, fell sound asleep. When they were in the midst of the Sea of Galilee a terrific storm burst upon them. The Galilean fishermen in the boat had been out in many a gale on this lake, but never had they experienced one so terrible as this. In spite of their frenzied bailing, the water was gaining on them. Panic laid hold on the hearts of the landsmen first of all. From them it spread, like a plague, to the fishermen, for fear is always infectious. Through all the excitement and terror Jesus lay asleep. Finally some one roused Him, crying, "Master, carest thou not that we perish?"

Now we must remember that Jesus was not a sailor. He probably had never been taught how to steer a ship in a stormy sea. He was a carpenter. Yet, when He stood up in that fishing-boat, such a look of confidence and peace was on His face that the fishermen began to wonder why they were afraid. One brave man, whether in a building on fire or in a storm at sea, can often shame a panic-stricken crowd out of their cowardice. Quietly the Master turned to the storm and chided it. He did this not because He feared the storm, but for the effect upon His companions. Then, almost in the same breath, He rebuked His disciples, saying, "Why are ye so fearful? How is it that ye have no faith?"

Now if we can discover the secret of Jesus' courage in the

[9] St. Mark IV:35-41.

face of danger and death, it may be that we can lay hold upon a principle that will preserve us from fear.

An inadequate interpretation has been given, for generations, to the Master's words. Most commentators declare that the reason He was disappointed in the disciples was because they should have known that the boat would not sink, that God would assuredly preserve their lives. Calvin, along with many other Christian teachers, accepts this explanation. He says that the disciples should have known that, while the humanity of Jesus was asleep, His divinity was awake, and that He would never have let them go to the bottom. Even so recent a writer as D. S. Cairns[10] says, "There was no reason for alarm; they would neither sink nor drown."

Let me say, at once, that I cannot accept this interpretation. It is too superficial, too cheap. Tens of thousands of men and women have gone down to a watery grave in the very hour that they cried to God to save them. In 1912, when the *Titanic* was sunk by an iceberg, it carried to their death in the Atlantic one thousand, five hundred and thirteen people. Were there none among these who prayed that God would deliver them from death?

There are countless situations in which the power of Christian faith is manifested not by the way in which it gives us deliverance from pain and death, but by the manner in which it enables us to transcend these evils and be superior to them. In certain circumstances a prayer for deliverance may be irrational and utterly selfish. Instead we ought to be praying for courage and faith to face whatever eventualities may await us. It was the lack in the disciples of these spiritual qualities that disappointed Jesus.

When He said to His disciples, "How is it that ye have no faith?" He was expressing His disappointment in them *because they were afraid*; because they had allowed themselves to be stampeded by fear. Jesus meant that if they had possessed true faith in God they would not have been afraid of the threat

[10] *The Faith That Rebels.*

of physical death. They would have been sustained by the assurance that, even though their bodies had found a resting-place on the bottom of the Lake of Gennesaret, their souls would have been secure in the keeping of God. It is altogether likely, too, that the peril in which they found themselves was due just as much to the fact that they had become paralyzed by fear as it was to the storm that raged around them. In Jesus' own case, we cannot fail to observe His utter indifference to the fate of His physical body because His goal was wholly a spiritual one. He tried to impart this outlook to His disciples when He said to them, "Be not afraid of them that kill the body, and after that have no more that they can do."[11]

The faith that Jesus had sought in His disciples is manifested in the life of Sir Wilfred Grenfell of the Labrador. In his autobiography[12] he tells us of the day on which he found himself drifting out into the Atlantic Ocean, on a little pan of ice, without food, without means of lighting a fire, and with only his dogs beside him. He was momentarily in danger of freezing to death. In order to save his life, he killed three of his dogs and skinned them, wrapping their furs around his own body. All night long he spent on that ice-pan. When morning broke he was miles out at sea. He hoped to call attention to his plight by means of signals. Using the frozen legs of the dogs tied together for a flag-pole, he fastened his shirt to the top of it and waved it frantically. Hour by hour he held aloft this improvised flag, without any result. Finally he became reconciled to death. These are his own words:

> "I can honestly say that from first to last not a single sensation of fear crossed my mind. My own faith in the mystery of immortality is so untroubled that it now seemed almost natural to be passing to the portal of death from an ice-pan. Quite unbidden, the words of the old hymn kept running through my head:

[11] Luke XII :4.
[12] *The Story of a Labrador Doctor*, Hodder & Stoughton, Ltd., London, England.

My God, my Father, while I stray
Far from my home on life's rough way,
Oh, teach me from my heart to say,
Thy will be done."

Snow-blinded, with hands and feet frozen, Dr. Grenfell was finally rescued by fishermen who had seen his signals as they looked out from distant cliffs.

How heartily Jesus would have approved the faith of that courageous man! Grenfell knew that there was no reason for fear. Even though the Atlantic should become "his vast and wandering grave," he would, as he himself expressed it, "go on living elsewhere" with ampler opportunities of service in the larger Life.

The Christian faith does not promise us immunity from the troubles that afflict mankind. Rather it is the means by which we may transcend them. On the night of His betrayal Jesus assured His disciples that there was trouble in store for them. "In the world," He said, "ye shall have tribulation." The root meaning of the word "tribulation" is to thrash or to beat. So the Master is telling the disciples that they will be beaten by the flail of adversity, that they will experience distresses and persecutions in the world, but He added, "Be of good cheer, I have overcome the world."[13]

No one who truly believes in God and has drawn upon the resources of confidence and peace that come from fellowship with Him will ever be mastered by fear. St. Paul utters the same defiant challenge to the tribulations of the world as did Jesus. He does not suggest that Christian faith is a sort of "safety first" or that it enables us to escape from life's difficulties. Indeed, he enumerates the trials that await us: "tribulation," "distress," "persecution," "famine," "nakedness," "peril," "sword." But he adds, "In all these things we are more than conquerors through him that loved us."[14] We are "super-

[13] St. John XVI :33.
[14] Romans VIII :35, 37.

conquerors" not because we have found a way of dodging life's tragedies, but because we have obtained the secret of triumphing over them.

This thought is expressed clearly and succinctly by John MacMurray in his book, *Freedom in the Modern World*.[15]

> "To the man who is afraid of poverty, it (the religion of Christ) does not say: 'God will save you from losing your money.' It says: 'Suppose you do lose your money, what is there to be afraid of in that?' If it is the fear of suffering and death that haunts you, real religion says, 'Yes, of course you will suffer and of course you will die, but there is nothing to be afraid of in that.' It does not say, as all false religion and false idealism does in effect: 'Shut your eyes to things you are afraid of; pretend that everything is for the best in the best of all possible worlds; and there are ways and means of getting the divine powers to your side, so that you will be protected from the things you are afraid of. They may happen to other people, but God will see to it that they don't happen to you.' On the contrary, true religion says, 'Look the facts you are afraid of in the face; see them in all their brutality and ugliness; and you will find, not that they are unreal, but that they are not to be feared.' "

In the early part of this chapter I quoted from Professor J. A. Hadfield's book, *Psychology and Morals*. There is one sentence in that quotation which is noteworthy: "The greatest fear of civilized man is himself."

That is why you are afraid. All of the anxieties that are wrecking the happiness of men and women in modern life— fear of unpopularity, fear of being a failure, fear of people, fear of unemployment, fear of poverty, fear of loneliness, fear of the dark, fear of illness, fear of death, are projected fears of ourselves. Our greatest problem is self-mastery. When we have conquered ourselves, we are masters of all the ills that threaten us. Then, even though we may make mistakes and

[15] D. Appleton-Century Company, publishers, New York.

suffer misfortunes, we will not be utterly cast down. Confidence and courage are given to us by the knowledge that in the end we shall conquer. As the poet sings:

"There is no storm but this
Of your own cowardice
  That braves you out.
You are the storm that mocks
Yourselves; you are the rocks
  Of your own doubt:
Besides this fear of danger, there's no danger here;
And he that here fears danger, does deserve his fear."

But how shall we attain self-mastery?

President Conant, addressing the graduates at the Harvard commencement exercises, referred to "the devastating effects of fear" and urged "the necessity of evolving a solid philosophy of life which will enable you, as educated men, to face the future unafraid."

When first I read this statement I was reminded of a visit I had paid to one of my parishioners in a large New York hospital. He was recovering from a serious and painful operation during which he had gone down to the very gates of death. Peering at me through a mass of bandages, this man, who is a university graduate and head of one of the greatest commercial organizations in this country, said, "Since I came to this hospital I have made a discovery that I shall not forget as long as I live. It is this: when a man comes up against the real issues of life and death he needs something more than a philosophy of life—he needs a faith."

I do not know how much content Dr. Conant would put into his words "a solid philosophy of life," but I know that a philosophy of life which is not undergirded by faith, far from being a firm foundation on which to build, is but treacherous shifting sand.

I seriously doubt whether anything short of faith in God will enable us "to face the future unafraid." Faith in God gives meaning to both life and death. It sends us forth to grapple with our most baffling problems in the confidence that a solution exists nearer than we are wont to think, are we but able to recognize and utilize it.

Faith in God strengthens our morale and enables us to see, to value highly, and to use our own inner resources in conjunction with the power of God. This state of high morale contrasts with the low state in which either or both the appropriate fears and the inappropriate anxieties surge up, scattering one's best resolutions and all of one's self-confidence.

God remains unshakable, while for the most part all is flux in man; but he who is able to hold fast to faith in God retains his own confidence in himself and, despite the evidence that would seem to mock his hopes, he believes that the power of God does and will prevail. This confidence counteracts any fear, be it appropriate or inappropriate to reality, and gives to one an abiding serenity and peace.

How often the Bible speaks of this glad consummation:

> "Thou wilt keep him in perfect peace, whose mind is stayed on thee."[16]
>
> "I sought the Lord, and he heard me, and delivered me from all my fears."[17]
>
> "There is no fear in love; but perfect love casteth out fear: because fear hath torment. He that feareth is not made perfect in love."[18]

[16] Isaiah xxvi:3.
[17] Psalm xxxiv:4.
[18] I John iv:18.

v. *The Sex Problems of Youth*

"That there should be no schism in the body; but that the members should have the same care one for another."

—I Corinthians xii:25

"For this cause shall a man leave father and mother, and shall cleave to his wife: and they twain shall be one flesh.
Wherefore they are no more twain, but one flesh."

—St. Matthew xix:5, 6

"Blessed are the pure in heart: for they shall see God."

—St. Matthew v:8

"Finally, brethren, whatsoever things are true, whatsoever things are honest, whatsoever things are just, whatsoever things are pure, whatsoever things are lovely, whatsoever things are of good report; if there be any virtue, and if there be any praise, think on these things."

—Philippians iv:8

IN EVERY parish, among the problems brought to the attention of the pastor are some which are frankly and unquestionably sexual problems, and of all the others brought to him few are completely devoid of a sexual reference. In other words, contained in many personal problems is at least some phase of a sexual problem. It is inevitable that an instinct as powerful as sex should permeate every area of the lives of men and women. It is extremely difficult to define or limit so protean an instinct and it seems only reasonable to assume that it will emerge in some form or other in most of the problems that the minister meets. If he does not meet with such cases it is not because they do not exist in his parish, but it is either that he has not sufficiently gained the confidence of his people for them to come to him with their problems or that he is unaware of the obvious and the disguised forms of sexual activity.

The minister who has adequately disciplined himself listens to confession of every variety of sexual activity without any embarrassment whatsoever either in himself or in those who come to confide in him.

It is most important that the pastor should have an understanding of the facts of sexual activities, not only those that may be classified as normal, but also those which are frequently described as abnormal or perversions. Only then is he able adequately to minister to those who come to him for help.

Every problem in the realm of sex should be rated according to its nearness to or divergence from normal sexual relations. There is no expression of mutual love between a man and a woman that is so complete and so satisfying as their normal sexual intercourse when they are in love with each other and bound together happily by marital ties. Such a relationship is not to be thought of on the mere physical plane, for it is a union that

97

is not only physical, but also mental and spiritual. It is not merely a physical union of two personalities, but it is the blending of two personalities into one, physically, mentally, and spiritually. It is a union as complete as that of two rivers that meet and mingle their waters as they run towards the sea. Jesus quoting the ancient book of Genesis[1] emphasized this aspect of the relationship of man and wife when he said:

> "For this cause shall a man leave father and mother, and shall cleave to his wife: and they twain shall be one flesh.
> "Wherefore they are no more twain, but one flesh. . . ."[2]

It is a holy and beautiful relationship carried out on a high moral plane, approved by human society and blessed of God. It is a happy, gratifying, beautiful experience.

A significant fact which a New York psychiatrist has pointed out is that universally man recognizes this sexual union of two married persons happily in love with each other as the only gratifying sexual relationship. He declared that he had talked with people faithful to their marriage vows and to those guilty of infidelity, to the chaste and to those who practised vice, to those who regarded sex as sacred as well as to prostitutes, and in every instance they all freely acknowledged that normal sexual intercourse between a husband and wife, married happily and lovingly to each other, is the only relationship which is really gratifying and the ideal sexual experience.

A happy and normal sexual relationship in marriage radiates happiness into all spheres of life and it enables those who enjoy it to be *en rapport* with their friends and with their associates, with mankind and with God.

Physicians inform us that, in the normal sexual relationship, there are three stages: first, the preliminary stage of love-making by conversation, caresses, kisses, and other expressions of affection and excitation; secondly, the actual sexual union reaching a simultaneous climax; thirdly, the aftermath of the

[1] Genesis II :24.
[2] St. Matthew XIX :5, 6.

sexual embrace characterized by inexpressible peace, relaxation, and happiness, with the sharing of thoughts, conversations, and plans for the future.

With this normal sexual relationship in mind the pastor will observe that most of the problems which have arisen in the lives of his parishioners are due to deviations from this normal and natural experience, such as masturbation, "petting," homosexuality, promiscuity. No matter how people who practise abnormal sex relations boast of their accomplishments they are, nevertheless, deeply conscious of a feeling of limitation and guilt. They know that their conduct lacks the approval of society, that it is a violation of moral standards, and that it is contrary to the laws of the Creator, which are built into the very structure of the universe and of human life. Their acts are accompanied and followed by a feeling of disgust with themselves and others and a deep sense of frustration. These feelings often produce neuroses and inner tensions which reach out and affect every segment of the life of the individuals concerned. All sex relations other than that of the normal intercourse of two married people in love with each other are evidences of a frustration already experienced and are but devaluated pleasures that inevitably lead to further emptiness and insipidity.

The pastor who has gained the confidence of the young people of his parish and who is wise in dealing with human problems is able oftentimes to preserve them from disaster. Let us look at some of the blind alleys into which youth oftentimes strays, dealing first of all with the one which will most frequently come to the pastor's attention.

As soon as I heard the tone of Frank's voice on the telephone that morning I knew something had gone seriously amiss with him.

"I want to talk with you just as soon as possible," he said. "I am in terrible trouble."

I made an appointment with him for two o'clock that afternoon. In the meantime I found myself wondering what could have happened to disturb so profoundly this quiet-mannered boy. It was easy for me to picture him as he looked when first

I met him, six months before. He was a tall, square, good-looking, fair-haired lad of seventeen and stood at least three inches higher than his father.

"My son Frank is going to college in the city and will be attending your church," his father, a well-known business man, had said.

His son had smiled shyly and extended his hand in greeting with a likeable sincerity. After that day I met him on several occasions, but we had never had a long or intimate conversation.

At two o'clock sharp Frank was ushered into the consulting-room.

"I am very sorry to have to trouble you, sir," he said, apologetically, "but I have been nearly desperate and must speak with some one."

As he talked his face was averted and he kept his eyes on the floor.

"At Christmas I failed in three out of six examinations and I am sure that I can't possibly make the grade this spring. Father is terribly hurt about it because his hopes are set on me. You see," he added, "I am an only child and he has always looked to me to succeed him."

There was a long and painful pause.

"What seems to be the matter?" I enquired.

"I couldn't tell you, sir," he replied in seeming contradiction of his earlier words. "I couldn't bring myself to tell any one. It's quite impossible."

"Well, Frank," I said, encouragingly, "I have had interviews with a great many people and I don't believe that there is anything you could tell me here today that some one has not told me before. I think that I have listened to nearly everything in the whole range of human frailties and sins."

"No, sir," Frank continued, "I am certain that you have never heard a story like mine. No one ever got as low as I have. There's really no hope for me."

"Well, Frank," I said, "I cannot help you unless you are willing to confide in me. Everything that passes between us here will be kept in inviolate confidence. Nothing will ever be repeated except with your consent."

"But, sir, I cannot tell you how low I have sunk," he said. "It's just too terrible for words."

"Then why did you come to me today?" I asked.

"I have to talk with some one or I shall go mad," was his reply.

I looked at the sad-faced youth who sat before me and, realizing that somehow I must get to the root of the matter, I suddenly asked him,

"How long ago did you commence this habit?"

Without looking up he answered, "Five years ago."

"You were about twelve years of age then, I take it."

"Yes, sir," he replied.

"Do you still practise it?" I asked.

"Not in the last couple of months," was his response. Then he continued, "But the shame of the thing has nearly driven me to distraction. I shall never be able to get it out of my mind. I have prayed about it for years. I keep thinking of it all the time so that I am unable to study and I know that I shall fail again in the final examinations."

"Would you be surprised," I asked him, "if I were to tell you that scores of boys of your age and many older men have made the same confession to me that you have made today?"

"It can't be possible," he replied, looking up quickly for the first time.

"It is not only possible," I answered, "but it is a fact that tens of thousands of boys have experimented, for longer or shorter periods of time, with the habit that has distressed you so much. It is called masturbation by physicians."

The light of hope sprang up in the eyes of this lad, when he learned that he was not the solitary, depraved creature which he had imagined himself to be.

I took down from a shelf in my library a book entitled *Manual of Psychiatry*,[3] by Dr. Aaron J. Rosanoff. "Here is a well-known medical textbook," I said. "Now read what it says on

[3] John Wiley & Sons, Inc., publishers, New York.

this page which deals with 'Sexual Psychopathies.'" This is what he read:

> "Masturbation is also very prevalent, and more so in the male sex, occurring in at least 90 per cent of males and 65 per cent of females. It starts as a rule earlier in females—between the ages of five and eleven years in nearly half the cases; whereas in males it starts between the ages of twelve and seventeen years in three-fourths of the cases. It is generally discontinued in early adult life when maturity of sexual constitution is attained, a deep interest in the opposite sex develops, and with it an instinctive feeling that masturbation is 'not right.' . . . Under the influence of quack literature and the prevailing exaggerated notions concerning masturbation, an 'inferiority complex' develops, giving rise to depression, discouragement, apprehension, and a sense of deep humiliation, and resulting in some cases in impairment of the individual's general efficiency in life."

When Frank had finished reading these words, there was an expression on his face that one might expect to see on the face of a condemned criminal who had suddenly been granted a reprieve.

I explained to the boy that according to the sanest psychiatric and medical testimony the damage done to him was not by the physical act but rather by the fact that he had continued the practice while believing that he was ruining his health and offending God. As a result it had created inner tensions and conflicts which made him feel that God had forsaken him. I told him that he had never understood what was the goal of a complete and normal sexual experience in the marriage relationship and that the habit, which he had been practising, if persisted in across the years, would make it very difficult for him to give a satisfactory sexual experience to his wife. He would have to unlearn the habit pattern he had been building up through the years, otherwise he would secure his gratification so quickly that his wife would be sexually starved.

As Frank gave me more and more of his confidence he told me that he had been lonesome for his father and envious of the boys whose dads came to see them frequently and shared their interests and their problems. It had given him more satisfaction than he was ready to admit when he discovered how deeply his father was hurt by his failure at Christmas. Unconsciously Frank had been working towards an even greater failure in the spring.

I showed the boy that both his masturbation and his failure in examinations were "bids" for his father's friendship, attention, and love and suggested that there were more direct and serviceable ways of attaining this end.

Even such a widely known author as Dr. John Rathbone Oliver[4] seems to overlook the fact that autoerotism is oftentimes an effect rather than a cause. He says,

> "Every time he drops back into his old habits what is he doing? Physically he is doing nothing harmful. But from a mental standpoint he is constantly breaking his word to himself. He is doing something that he promised, that he resolved not, to do. Naturally this undermines one of youth's most precious possessions, his self-confidence. Little by little he loses his sense of self-confidence—that power to direct his own life, which is such a necessity for the young man in his early manhood. Robbed of it, he begins to develop one of the most poisonous, one of the most handicapping, mental habits in existence, a sense of inferiority. And this habitual sense of inferiority is ten thousand times more serious than all the autoerotic habits in the world. It will follow him through life, will make him shy, self-conscious, distrustful of himself, envious of others. It may make a complete failure out of a life that should have been successful and valuable. These are the real dangers of autoerotism."

It seems to me that Dr. Oliver has missed a vital point. He

[4] *Psychiatry and Mental Health.* Charles Scribner's Sons, publishers, New York.

depicts masturbation almost wholly as a cause, whereas generally it is the other way round. As in the case of the boy to whom I have referred, masturbation is one of the many variable results of a previously existing lack of self-confidence and lack of confidence in others. It is not the cause of inferiority, though, of course, it deepens the feeling of inadequacy. He who has complete self-confidence does not habitually masturbate.

I pointed out to Frank that he had failed to make a constructive use of prayer. Each day, as he prayed about the habit that had enchained him, he set it directly in the forefront of his consciousness, thus accomplishing more harm than good.

"Let your next prayer to God," I said to him, "be one of thanksgiving for complete deliverance not only from this habit, but also from all fear of its consequences, and then forget about the whole business." I read to him Paul's references, in one of his epistles, to the organs of the body :[5]

"For the body is not one member, but many.

"If the foot shall say, Because I am not the hand, I am not of the body; is it therefore not of the body?

"And if the ear shall say, Because I am not the eye, I am not of the body; is it therefore not of the body?

"If the whole body were an eye, where were the hearing? If the whole were hearing, where were the smelling?

"But now hath God set the members every one of them in the body, as it hath pleased him.

"And if they were all one member, where were the body?

"But now are they many members, yet but one body.

"And the eye cannot say unto the hand, I have no need of thee: nor again the head to the feet, I have no need of you.

"Nay, much more those members of the body, which seem to be more feeble, are necessary.

"And those members of the body, which we think to be less honourable, upon these we bestow more abundant honour; and our uncomely parts have more abundant comeliness.

[5] I Corinthians xii :14-26.

"For our comely parts have no need: but God hath tempered the body together, having given more abundant honour to that part which lacked:

"That there should be no schism in the body; but that the members should have the same care one for another.

"And whether one member suffer, all the members suffer with it; or one member be honoured, all the members rejoice with it."

"Now," I said, "we do not change the sense of this passage one iota if we substitute 'sex organs' for 'foot' or 'hand' or 'eye,' for it declares that:

" 'God hath set the members every one of them in the body as it hath pleased him.'

"We can paraphrase it to read:

" 'And the eye cannot say to the sex organs
I have no need of thee. . . .'

"You must not and you need not think, Frank," I said, "that there is anything shameful about any part of the body, for every organ of the body has been fashioned by the Creator and has an honourable function to fulfil."

"I never thought of it that way before," Frank interjected.

"Remember, too," I added, "that sex feelings in themselves are not sinful. Sex hunger is not a bit more wicked than hunger for food. If you did not possess these urges it would be an indication that there was something abnormal about you. Your trouble arose from the fact that you misdirected a perfectly natural and God-given instinct and had no goal."

I reminded him of Jesus' parable about the man whose house had been inhabited by a demon. He drove out the intruder and left his dwelling swept and garnished but empty. Then the evil spirit returned and, finding the house empty, brought with him seven spirits more wicked than himself and they entered and made their dwelling-place there, so that the last state of the man was worse than the first. I cautioned Frank to insure that the rooms of his soul should not be left unoccupied when undesirable tenants had been expelled, that the Spirit of Christ should be admitted to every segment of his life and welcomed daily as a beloved guest.

Before Frank left the study we knelt together in prayer and he thanked God for the deliverance that had been given to him from all his fears and also for the assurance of victory in the future.

I reminded Frank of Professor William James' comparison of a man endeavouring to learn new habits with a person winding up into a ball a quantity of twine strewn about the floor of a room. If he should accidentally drop the ball when the task was uncompleted there would be no sense in his sitting down and bewailing the fact. He should realize that while the twine had unrolled a bit he had already made good progress and, picking up the ball, would go to work again winding up the string with undiminished patience and hope. I urged him not to be unduly discouraged should a time come when he slipped back momentarily into the old habit. He had committed the whole matter to God and should remember that God would understand and help him.

Frank walked out of the church house with his head held high and it should hardly be necessary to add that he did not fail in his spring examinations.

I wrote a letter to his father and, without revealing any of the confidences that the boy had given me, I made it clear to his parent that Frank needed a larger measure of his father's companionship and affection.

One of the most distressing features of this case is the fact that the boy's father had left his son in colossal ignorance of one of the most vital functions of life. He had established a business that was continent-wide in its scope and had given, without stint, of his time and his energy to its promotion, but he had had no time to talk with his son of the distressing problems that were nearly driving him to distraction. The larger the responsibility that a father carries the greater is the danger that he will allow his business or professional interests to stand between him and his children. Indeed, this is a peril that every father faces.

One does not have to look far to find abundant illustration of the damaging effects of parental neglect and parental ignorance. The authors of *Child Guidance*[6] relate the following incident:

"A young man nineteen years of age was taken to a hospital for nervous diseases. He was a member of the college football team. During a game he wrenched his back. He was taken from the field and the next day was unable to walk. They brought him to a local hospital, but a careful examination failed to reveal any physical injury. His condition seemed to be due to some emotional state.

"At the special hospital it was found that, when he was ten years of age, he was discovered by his father masturbating. His father told him that the habit would cause his backbone to soften and decay. He masturbated infrequently from the age of ten to fifteen and then stopped the practice completely. But the fear was with him always that he had irreparably injured his back. Every time he felt a pain there he believed that the degeneration of the spine had begun. When he became injured on the football field he lapsed into hopelessness and felt that death was near.

"After three days' treatment the boy was discharged completely well and happy that the burden had at last been lifted."

On one occasion a father who had come to me for advice on the matter of sex information said:

"I have discovered that my boy has developed some bad sex habits. What should I tell him about them?"

When I suggested that he should explain to his son that the physical damage done by the habit was relatively slight and that he should earnestly seek the reason why the boy had devel-

[6] *Child Guidance*, by Smiley Blanton, B.S., M.D., and Margaret Blanton. The D. Appleton-Century Company, New York.

oped the practice in the first place, the father broke in impatiently,

"But if I told him that, he would never be master of himself. I've got to frighten him."

I explained to the father that the first step in the emancipation of the victim came with the assurance that irreparable physical and mental damage had not already been done.

Dr. W. F. Robie, after thirty years' experience with thousands of cases, writes as follows:[7]

> ". . . Another statement hard to believe, but nevertheless proved true by myself in scores of cases, is this: if one convincingly tells a person who is trying to overcome the practice of masturbation and worrying over the supposed evil effects of it, the truth that no harm can arise from this except from the worry concerning it, there is not only immediate relief from all nervous symptoms, but a diminution in the frequency or even a cessation of the practice."

Another blind alley or abnormal sexual relationship that the minister will frequently meet is that which is colloquially called "petting."

A third-year student of arts, in a distressful mental state, wrote me for advice. I talked with him where he boarded.

"I don't know what is the matter with me," he said. "I seem to get started well enough at my studies, but I can't seem to finish them. After I have been working for a little while my nerves start to bother me and I go to pieces. I have been having a lot of headaches, too. I don't think I have a chance of making my grade in the spring examinations."

"What seems to be the greatest fault in your habits of study?" I asked him.

"Well, I don't seem capable of keeping at a subject for any length of time. When I've made only a commencement I get all

[7] "Sex and Life," pp. 231, 232. Rational Life Publishing Company, 205 William Street, Ithaca, N. Y.

jittery and have to turn to another subject in my course, but I do no better there."

"What you've just told me, Russell," I said, "looks to me like a habit pattern. Look at the wall paper. You will see that there is a design which runs through it all. It is repeated over and over again. Now you might assume that the wall paper behind you has the same design and, if you will look behind you, you will see that it has."

"Yes, that's quite true," he said. "The same pattern appears everywhere on the wall."

"Doesn't that suggest anything to you?" I asked.

"I'm afraid I can't see what you're driving at," he replied.

"Well, if I am right in my belief that you have revealed a habit pattern in what you have told me about your studies, the same pattern should be appearing elsewhere in areas of your life that you haven't discussed with me. If it appears in that part of your life that you have laid open to my gaze it is likely to be repeated in other segments of your character that you have not revealed to me. Now tell me about some of these other things," I suggested.

"Well, I might as well get the whole business off my chest," he replied. "I've got into a kind of a mess with my girl. For a good part of the winter I have been having 'heavy dates' with her. She is a co-ed at the university where I am taking my course."

By a "heavy date" he explained that he had experienced orgasms without a complete normal sexual relationship. In other words, his sex episode ended at the first of the three stages described by physicians. He achieved this inadequate goal through kissing, fondling, caressing, and embracing his companion. As often as four times a week they had engaged in petting parties.

The day following, at my suggestion, his girl friend, Mabel, came to see me. She was extremely tense and talkative and she, too, seemed to be suffering from nervous strain. She told me that her relations with her fellow student had been even more unsatisfactory than his had been with her. She had not achieved the release from sexual tension that had been his experience and as a result was in an even more tense condition than he. They were deeply in love with each other, but because of the fact of the secrecy of their relationships an accompanying sense of guilt and shame robbed these young people of peace of mind and spirit. They felt that their sex relationships were carried on on a plane that was low socially and morally.

In an interview with both of them together I explained to them the facts of a normal sex relationship and pointed out that they were unfitting themselves physically for a normal and happy marriage in that they were training themselves in ways that were not only not useful to them in marriage, but were actually so unserviceable that they would later have to be un-learned.

"The nervous tension that has troubled both of you so much," I explained to him, "is due to the fact that night after night you have been going through all the exciting preliminaries of a complete sexual embrace with the understanding that you would go thus far and no farther. You have subjected yourself and this girl to an intense emotional strain which has already left its mark upon both of you."

I quoted to them the lines written by George Macdonald:

> "Alas, how easily things go wrong!
> A sign too deep, or a kiss too long.
> There follows a mist and a weeping rain,
> And life is never the same again."

The manner in which they were carrying on their sex expression militated against their happiness and a habit pattern had been established, which they would have to break down before marriage could give them the fullest possible spiritual union in one of the holiest relationships that one human being can have with another.

I talked to them of Jesus' teaching on marriage and of His ideal of the complete blending of the physical, mental, and spiritual in holy married love.

"You see, sir," the youth interjected, "we love one another

dearly and, while we didn't feel that we should express that love in a full sex relationship before marriage, we thought that petting was a legitimate substitute."

"Well, tell me, did you find from your own experience that it was 'legitimate,' Russell?" I asked.

"You know the answer to that and the same holds good for it as a substitute," he responded.

"One of your major troubles is due to the fact that you have been involved in something for which you could not have the sanction either of society or of God," I observed. "What are the prospects of early marriage of you and Mabel? If you can arrange that, even at a sacrifice, you will have a legitimate relationship that carries with it the sanction of society and of God."

"We shall have to wait for about a year," Russell replied, "and that's that."

"Well, you came to me because you are feeling miserable. This has to do with your experimentation. Would you be willing to try another kind of experiment I have to offer?"

The faces of both young people lighted up.

"I know others who have tried your kind of experiment and have found it empty and unsatisfactory. I know, too, people who are married and have had all the merely sexual relations they desired and they similarly found them empty and unsatisfactory. You people certainly have heard of divorce, but probably haven't thought that you are potential divorcers. Why don't you plan now either to separate, because you have found this kind of sex life unsatisfactory, or else to enrich your companionship so definitely that after marriage much more will exist in your intimacies than the sexual. You've got the beginnings of divorce in you right now in that you are accumulating discontents and misery by your continuing the kind of experimentation you've been doing. I am asking you to accumulate contentments and happiness as a background for the enjoyment of a sexual relationship in marriage approved by God and your fellow-men. Just sex alone will not make any two people happy. You will need also an enriched and enriching congeniality as you go on together through life."

"I can see clearly how one could develop that congeniality in mutual secular interests, but where does religion come in? We have agreed upon the first, though we haven't done much about it, but we have never even mentioned the second. Wouldn't it be enough to carry on our secular interests without religion?" asked Mabel.

"People have tried it, of course, without any spiritual mutuality," I said. "Other people who have had some spiritual congeniality have lost it, drifted apart secularly and divorced. But I have never known a married couple with a spiritual mutuality of sufficient strength that they regularly prayed together at home, who became divorced. Think about that, will you?" I looked at Mabel. She nodded assent.

And turning to Russell, I asked, "And you, too?"

He seemed not to hear my question, though I knew that he had been listening. Both of them appeared oblivious of my presence as Russell took Mabel's hand and his eyes communed with hers in a language not translatable into words.

Then, as we three bowed our heads in prayer I knew that two young people had found their way out of one of life's blind alleys and had set their feet on the white highway of God's will, that leads to contentment and peace.

The preservation of chastity is a problem for many unmarried young people. For some there has been little or no temptation for a sexual experience with anybody. Occasionally there are individuals who take the attitude that chastity means sexual abstinence between two people of the opposite sex and that any indulgence of a man and a woman leading to orgasms, not from a full sexual relationship, does not itself violate chastity. Likewise there are those who consider that the achievement of a sex climax with someone of the same sex or by oneself alone may be classified as chastity. This is strange and mistaken reasoning. One sometimes finds even celibacy defined in the foregoing terms.

When a man and a woman of any age have a strong attraction toward each other and desire a sexual relationship and are yet unable to have it in the marriage tie, if the temptation conflicts with an equally strong desire to retain chastity in completeness, both while they are together and when they are apart, their dilemma is oftentimes brought to the attention of a pastor.

A great deal was written a little time ago about the necessity of young people experimenting in sex relations. Trial marriage was a popular topic of conversation. Some of these writers sought to make people believe that a marriage was almost certainly doomed to failure if the contracting couple had not proved their suitability to each other by previous sex relations. Physicians and psychiatrists are pointing out today that this is a mistaken idea. Most frequently a pre-marital sex experience with one another, by the parties to a marriage, makes for discord rather than happiness in the new relationship. They have already spoiled for themselves what ought to be the culmination of their romance. The sexual embrace can never bring to them all that it is normally intended to convey of an unspeakable heightening of happiness. They find themselves face to face with the difficult personal adjustments that must be made in the marriage relationship without the corresponding compensations of which they have already deprived themselves. They are liable, also, to be suspicious of each other, knowing that each holds to the creed of sex freedom. They lack that mutual trust which is the only sure basis on which to build a stable marriage relationship.

Dr. Alfred Adler, in common with many other physicians and psychiatrists, brands as utterly false the notion that it is necessary for young people to have sex relations in the interests of their health. There is no sound medical basis for this contention, says Dr. Adler. The cult of the post-war moral sophisticates, which taught that full expression must be given to the sex instincts, regardless of the consequences, is losing its appeal and chastity is once again coming into its own.

A young woman, who is a graduate of an American university, came to me for help in dealing with a problem that had emerged in her life. She said:

"I have come more than a thousand miles from my home, looking for work in New York. My father and mother were opposed to my leaving home, so were my two brothers, but I like to make my own decisions and besides they are having trouble enough to meet the financial burden of caring for those who are now at home, without having me on their hands as well. The only position I have been able to secure is that of saleslady in a New York department store. This gives me but two days' work each week. I find that it is impossible to support myself in this city on the wages that I receive. I am engaged to be married to a young man who has two more years to put in at college. His financial situation does not permit us to marry until after he has graduated and obtained a job, and I can get no help from home.

"Just as I was wondering what I could do about this matter I met a young man whom I had known several years ago in a social way. He asked me what I was doing in New York and I told him. He then wanted to know how much money I was receiving per week and where I lived, and I told him this, too. He is only five or six years older than I and is very wealthy and quite good-looking. When he had learned the facts about my situation in New York he said to me:

" 'That is no kind of way for a pretty girl like you to be living. I know what you would like. You want to have pretty clothes, to be able to see some shows, and to have a few square meals a week, which I don't think you have been getting. Now I am ready to give you all these things, to put you up in your own apartment with your own automobile and chauffeur. To be perfectly frank with you, it is a two-way proposition. I am not willing to do this for nothing. I shall expect you to be my mistress. You will be perfectly free to break off this relationship any time you please and I will see that you have plenty of money to get anything you want or to send some home to your people. I may tell you that you will not be the first mistress that

I have had. There is no hurry about this. Think it over and let me know your answer at your convenience.' "

At this point the young woman opened her purse and, taking out a card, glanced at it, saying:

"I have here his name, address, and telephone number." Continuing, she said, "I attended your church on Sunday morning and took Communion. When the service was over I felt that I simply had to talk with you. That is why I am here. Now tell me," she said, "what do you think I ought to do about this?"

I said to her, "What do you think you ought to do?"

"Well," she replied, "I didn't come to talk about my own ideas on the subject, if I have any. I came to get advice from you and I hope you are not going to disappoint me."

"I shall be very glad to help you all I can," I said, "but I still want an answer to my question. What do you think about this man's proposition?"

A slight flush of anger crept into her cheeks and she said:

"Is this the way you deal with people who come to you for counsel? If so, I am sorry I came. I had thought that you were always willing to give people advice and help, but since I am mistaken in this," she said, rising from her chair, "I might as well go."

"Now, just a moment," I said, reassuringly. "Sit down and I will explain what I mean."

She sat down.

"Please believe me when I say that I do want to help you. I asked what you thought about this man's offer because I know that you have some definite thoughts on the matter."

"How do you know that?" she asked.

"You told me that you like to decide for yourself. If you already believe that the proposition which this man has offered you is a desirable one, why did you not accept it? Why have you come to me? The very fact that you are here talking to me, a minister, shows that you have some very grave doubts about the advisability of your accepting his suggestions. Now I want you to tell me about these doubts. Why have you hesitated to accept his offer? Come, be perfectly frank with me."

"Well," she said, "in the first place, I know that he doesn't love me. I grant you he may be drawn to me by a physical attraction, but if he really loved me he wouldn't make the proposition to me that he has made, whereas my boy friend at college truly loves me and wants to marry me. The suggestion is repulsive to me that I should have sex relations with a man whom I do not love and who doesn't love me."

"Well, that is one reason. You must have some others."

"I think he is putting a price on something that cannot be valued in money," she continued. "If I accepted his offer I should feel that I had sold myself, that I had bartered something that is a priceless possession. I find that I have a growing dislike for this man for even suggesting that pretty clothes, dinner parties, an automobile, and money would be a satisfactory substitute to me for my self-respect and my sense of decency."

"That's fine," I said, encouragingly. "Have you any other reasons?"

"Yes," she said. "If I accepted this man's offer I should be betraying the love of the young man to whom I am engaged. I am certain that he is straight and he trusts me. I could never look him in the eye again if I were false to that trust. I should look forward with nothing but dread to the intimate relationships of marriage if I had already spoiled them for myself."

"Are these all the reasons you have for turning this man down?" I asked.

"No," she said, "I have a number of others but the most important of all is my faith in God. If I went with this man I should feel that I had turned my back upon God and broken His commandments. I don't feel that they are just orders imposed from without. For years I have felt that there is something within me that responds to the moral standards of the Bible. My mind acquiesces in them. They are approved by my intelligence. When I am wed to my *fiancé*, we shall be married in a church and we shall seek God's blessing on our marriage and on our home. I don't want a relationship with any man upon which I cannot ask God's blessing."

As she spoke these last words her lips trembled with emotion. There was silence for a moment and then I said:

"I agree with you in every point that you have made. I agree that you would be heading for tragedy and heartbreak if you became a mistress of this man. It is easy to see that everything that is fine within you revolts against the suggestion. I admire you for your convictions. Now may I ask what is your final decision?"

"I am going to tell him," she said, "that he can keep his pretty clothes and his dinner parties and his automobile and his money; that I would rather starve to death than accept his offer and I shall give him the reasons that I gave to you."

"By the way, whose reasons are those that you have gone over point by point?"

"They are mine," she said, simply.

"Are you sure that I haven't imposed them on you?"

"Certainly not," she replied. "They are my own ideas."

"That is true," I assented. "You had them before you came today but I have helped you to find out what they really are, so that you can carry them into action. I believe that each girl who has a problem like this to solve has at least some desire not to accept the easy way out but that she needs to declare herself on this point definitely to some one before she gets the courage to take action for the right. When spiritual force is added to secular determination one goes 'from strength to strength.'

"You came to me, a minister, knowing beforehand my point of view but before you came you were not at all aware how much of your own point of view was identical with mine. Now you are going out to act on your own convictions. . . ."

As the young woman said "Good-bye" there was something in the tone of her voice which indicated that a disturbing problem had been brought to a final and happy solution.

No minister can deal adequately with sex problems in the lives of his young people who does not keep constantly in mind the ideal relationship that is found only in a happy marriage. Sex experiences produced in ways which are not approved of or recommended by society, nor blessed by a minister of God, sometimes, but not always, evoke a momentary pleasure, but they are all followed closely by feelings of guilt, remorse, unworthiness, disgust with oneself and others, bitterness, hate, the need for punishment of oneself and of others, until health and happiness disappear and neurotic, unsocial and antisocial results ensue.

The individual who truly and happily loves another has little or no impulse to gratify himself alone sexually or to have illicit relationships with the one that is loved. To such a one the practice of masturbation, "petting," or other unsocial forms of sexual behaviour is an empty event, unsatisfactory and incomplete. Unpleasant reactions are inevitable because one has carried on to a climax an experience that cannot bring anything but some species of misery. A neurosis overtakes him as the result of disappointment and frustration.

One knows ahead of time, in all illicit sex relations, that his tendencies are toward something that is contrary to his own, his family's, society's, the church's and God's approval, and after having expressed his tendencies in action he feels that he has received the disapproval and punishment of his family, of society, his church, and God.

It is important to remember, however, that it is usually the frustrated individual who already feels inadequate who practises such sex experiments as masturbation, petting parties, homosexuality, adultery, or vice in any of its forms. Then, having indulged in what is doomed at the outset to be another frustration, he feels worse than ever and, feeling worse, indulges himself again, because his sexual activities are conducted primarily not for the pleasure which they afford, but as an outlet for psychic tensions which they invariably fail to relieve. Thus his sexual experience moves in a vicious circle, bringing an unsolved and steadily accentuated problem repeatedly to the fore in his life.

Marriage solves most of the problems localized in the normal sexual realm. But marriage does not, *ipso facto,* satisfy the yearnings and the need for social, mental, and spiritual union except in those husbands and wives who are able to unite in those ways with a mate. Husbands and wives who attain the greatest degree of union physically, mentally, and spiritually have worked to achieve it. Their success is not accidental. It is the result of the blending of spontaneity and loving, thoughtful planning.

Similarly, marriage is not a "cure" for anything. A marriage ceremony of itself does not cure a nasty disposition, unsocial, anti-social or perverted sexuality. Some people naïvely assume that marriage means a legalizing of sexual relations or is a means of relief from abnormal sex habits such as masturbation, petting, promiscuity, and the like. But if these habits have been persisted in over a long period, marriage may do little or nothing to remedy them and may mean that the happiness of two lives, instead of one, has been ruined. Such a view of marriage is merely a travesty of the reality and those who enter upon it on these terms alone are doomed to failure and disappointment to a greater or less degree.

At the same time it must be remembered that where early marriage is desired by the young people themselves, and where they are prepared to accept the responsibilities and obligations that it will involve, parents can render to them an incalculable service by removing the barriers that economic obstacles place in the way of their early union.

Thomas Chalmers, the Scottish preacher of the nineteenth century, and later Professor William James, wrote of the "expulsive power of a new affection." A truly happy sexual love between a husband and wife drives out with expulsive power many of the annoying troubles and worries that had previously distressed them. This is particularly true if their love is of a kind that is daily renewed in its free flowing spontaneity.

Over a long span of time marriage is not in itself necessarily a complete solution of one's need for merely physical sex relief because this relationship too produces its own species of problem. Not always are a husband and wife ready and eager at the same time for sexual relations. It may be that one is tired and the other rested; the one sick and the other exasperatingly well; the one returning from a trip sexually hungry and the other preoccupied with routine; the one without any worrisome responsibility and the other fretted by duty. Any or all of these possibilities may occur in the course of a normal marriage, so that, unless sexual relations from the beginning of a marriage are planned for understandingly and lovingly, they will degenerate into a source of discord and unhappiness.

A new problem emerges in the marital relationship for every old one left behind in the pre-marital state, therefore the greatest care should be exercised lest indulgence in abnormal sexual experimentation before marriage place an insuperable handicap upon two people's hope of happiness after they are united as man and wife.

For all those who must undergo the discipline of a period of waiting before marriage will be possible, as well as for those for whom marriage is but a far-distant goal, there remains the sublimation or redirection of the powerful forces of sex. The whole of life may be irradiated with a spiritual glow as these vital energies are directed to the accomplishment of high and worthy enterprises as they were in the life of Paul, Augustine, Francis of Assisi, Joan of Arc, Florence Nightingale, and a multitude of others, including Jesus Himself. Whether in the marriage relationship or outside it a disciplined sex life consecrated to God will engender the maximum happiness for ourselves and others and produce in ourselves a vital and harmonious personality. As the Talmud says:

> "The greater a man is the stronger are his passions but the pure and consecrated man makes of his passions a chariot for God."

VI. *Humiliation and Pride*

"Whosoever shall exalt himself shall be humbled; and whosoever shall humble himself shall be exalted."

—St. Matthew XXIII:12
(Revised Version)

"Be clothed with humility: for God resisteth the proud, and giveth grace to the humble.

"Humble yourselves therefore under the mighty hand of God, that he may exalt you in due time."

—I Peter v:5, 6

"If anyone imagines he is somebody, he is deceiving himself, for he is nobody; let everyone bring his own work to the test—then he will have something to boast about on his own account, and not in comparison with his fellows."

—Galatians vi:3, 4
(Moffatt's Translation)

"Whosoever therefore shall humble himself as this little child, the same is greatest in the kingdom of heaven."

—St. Matthew XVIII:4

A POPULAR topic of conversations in many drawing-rooms seems to be the "inferiority complex." Many people who possess a feeling of inadequacy are said to be suffering from an inferiority complex. The expression is bandied about with little regard for its real significance.

A complex has been defined as: "A group of ideas of spontaneous and emotional character associated by the individual with a particular subject, often indicating a kind of mental abnormality arising from repressed instincts or the like."[1]

A genuine experience of inferiority complex is one of many phases of mental abnormality, the extremes of which are met with relatively infrequently and quite frequently in slight degrees.

Humiliation is the term which, in religious parlance, would correspond to the term "inferiority" as it is used by the psychiatrist. Humiliation and pride are set over against each other, for, when one intensity is present in an individual, we look always for its opposite, present simultaneously or in disguise. If a man is blatant about his atheism, we expect to find in him a desire for belief in God. If he is constantly protesting his faith, we may look for an inclination to doubt. If he is suffering from impulses to suicide, we may expect to find in him a marked desire to live and to accomplish something in which he has been thwarted. If he evidences conceit, we may expect to find inferiority. If he is distressed by a feeling of humiliation, we may be sure that pride also is present.

The ideal in human character is the humble man who is neither overwhelmed with humiliation nor exalted with pride. Jesus said, "Whosoever shall exalt himself shall be humbled and whosoever shall humble himself shall be exalted."[2]

[1] Oxford Dictionary.
[2] St. Matthew XXIII:12. Revised Version.

Jesus is here saying that when a man sets himself up in boastful pride God will bring him low; but if a man humbles himself in the presence of God, seeking not to enhance his own glory but only to perform the Divine will, him will God exalt.

By "humbling" oneself Jesus does not mean that we should feel humiliation, and by being "exalted" He is not advocating pride. He is extolling humility, the only kind of human behaviour that can be truthfully designated "normal"—the golden mean between humiliation and pride.

St. Peter says: ". . . Be clothed with humility: for God resisteth the proud, and giveth grace to the humble. Humble yourselves therefore under the mighty hand of God, that he may exalt you in due time."[3] The apostle is not suggesting that we should constantly be grovelling in the presence of God. God does not desire men to come to him like abject slaves. But he who is humble in the presence of God will never feel humiliated in the presence of his fellow-men.

Ezekiel, the prophet, records[4] a vision of the glory of God during which he was overcome by a feeling of awe and fell upon his face. While he was bowed in the Divine Presence, he heard the voice of the Lord saying unto him: "Son of man, stand upon thy feet, and I will speak to thee."

When men have humbled themselves in the presence of God it is only that they may be able to stand upon their feet, to hear the voice of God and to look the world and their fellow-men in the face.

One sees quite frequently in human lives the damaging effects of a feeling of humiliation with its accompaniment of pride.

A series of letters from a young man, accompanied by corroborations from his mother, stated that he was almost at the height of a successful "career before the public," but that he was almost overwhelmed by inner feelings of inadequacy and unworthiness. He had confidence in himself only when he was before the public and got its praise and applause, and then he could move and speak with whatever tone of voice, gestures,

---

[3] I. Peter v:5, 6.
[4] Ezekiel 1:27-11:1.

and facial expression were appropriate. He was an actor who had played extensively in stock companies. He wrote of his entire satisfaction with himself when he was before the foot-lights and of his utter shyness, tongue-tiedness, awkwardness, and self-consciousness when offstage.

My first interview with him personally revealed the realities of his letter. He assured me he was a first-rate actor, even though as yet unrecognized, unacclaimed universally, but al-ways popular wherever he played. To show his versatility he listed his rôles and performed from several of them as if he were having an "audition" in my small consulting-room. He revealed what seemed to me a bit of exhibitionism and pleased-ness with himself. Then he stopped short as if waiting for ap-plause. But I did not applaud, for I was waiting for him to carry on spontaneously from his inner impulses.

He reacted with obvious embarrassment. His self-confidence vanished; he backed away from my desk both geographically and socially. This man of good presence, good looks, changed to one of countenance and posture that was as unprepossessing as his first was engrossing. His speech was halting, a bit stam-mering at times. His story came out piecemeal, spaced by silences, but its substance is as follows:

"I haven't any real right to come to you, sir, for I don't go to church regularly, though I belong to one. I went as a boy and I had a good start in religion from my mother and from a Sunday-school teacher. I heard your voice on the radio without knowing you were a minister. Something you said has brought me here. . . . It's nice of you to see me. I'm not worth your time and trouble, and yet, sir, I am—I'll prove it if you'll give me some help. I act on the stage and forget myself completely in my rôle—but you see I don't exist as myself then—I am somebody else. Then the rest of the time I'm on the sidelines watching someone else. I'm not part of the audience watching the unreality of the theatre. I am part of the unreality itself. But it's not even me acting. The me myself just hangs on the sideline, never participating, never enjoying life. . . . If I could only be like other people. I feel that I am both far above and far below the average, but that I am not at any time or place 'average' or 'regular.' "

"I should be interested to know how deeply this trouble is rooted in your life. Tell me some of the recollections of your early childhood," I said.

"As far back as I can remember I was pushed off to the edge of the group," he replied. "I remember one day standing with my mother on the front porch. It was Hallowe'en. Boys were playing pranks in the street and one of my older brothers came running up with a mask on his face and frightened me so that I ran into the house and looked out the window. I saw mother scolding the boys for teasing me. I remember, too, that I used to go down the street to play with two little girls who lived a few doors away, and my brothers jeered at me for playing with girls. I ran back to my mother, crying, and she took my part. I have always been proud of the fact that mother called me 'a good boy.'

"Another time two boys commenced to fight with one of my brothers and had him down on the ground. I went to his help, but my brother told me to mind my own business, that he could look after himself. I've always felt he was right—that he never has needed me and nobody else ever has, either. And I've never been able to take the side of anybody else—someone has always looked out for me."

I interrupted him here: "There are a couple of things I would like to bring to your attention immediately if I may break into your line of thought. It occurs to me that there is a similarity between the patterns of your earliest memories and of your problems today. What do you think of it?"

"I never had thought so," he responded, "but now that you speak of it, it does seem as though these memories are related to my present feelings of inadequacy."

"Isn't it significant," I said, "that now you have come to me to take your side. Your mother took your part. You watched her from the window scold the other boys and you *let* her do your fighting for you. You *let* her stand up for you. No, you *made* her do it for you and ever since you *make* some one else fight for you. You come asking me to help you. If I should let you, you would make *me* protect you from the difficulties of your existence and I would be a substitute for your mother and you would be no more than that same little boy who, scared by your brother's Hallowe'en mask, ran away crying and watched from inside the house. You see that, Mr. Blain, don't you? Contained in your coming to me today is this pattern of a boy running to his mother. I would only harm you if I help you on your terms. I do not consent to those terms. Nor do I consent to your making God a substitute for your mother."

"What! You turn me down, sir? And you a minister!" he rebuked me.

"Please!—notice exactly what I say. You are 'in character' at the moment, running true to type. Life-long, you find yourself in trouble, run away, look back from a position of safety to see your mother, or her substitute, protecting you. Do you see that the rôle of the little boy is important in the drama of your life and do you see how futile and unreligious it would be for you to go to God in a childish fashion. You do see the distinction, don't you, between childishness and child-likeness?"

"Yes, sir," he responded, "I do."

He told me, in response to a question from me, about his religious life. It paralleled, he volunteered, the rest of his life. He learned his prayers as a little boy and repeated them with his mother because she told him to do so; he went to church and to Sunday school at her direction, but none of it all meant anything to him directly. His mother answered any of his questions about God by saying he was too little a boy to explain to, but that when he grew up he would understand.

"But did you never have any feeling that God was near you, or watching you?" I asked him.

"Oh yes, whenever I did anything I was ashamed of I felt God was watching me. That was my own idea. But that is as far as I ever went on my own. I knew how my folks felt about the Bible and God, but I never felt those ways myself. I wish I could."

With his comment I opened a New Testament to I Corinthians 13:11 and gave it to him to read aloud. This is what he read:

> "When I was a child, I spake as a child, I understood as a child, I thought as a child: but when I became a man, I put away childish things."

He was silent for a moment and then he said:

"That's exactly the thing I ought to have done but haven't. That text certainly shows me up. I haven't put away childish things."

I impressed upon him that it was not Mr. Blain, the accomplished actor, grown up, who had been standing by, watching other people enjoy themselves but little Freddie who had never grown up; that he had been reproducing his boyhood pattern and that his relation to God also was still that of a little boy who continued to think of God as his mother had told him to. He had never thought of God as would a grown man.

"You say that as a boy you felt God's presence when you were doing wrong. Have you never realized that God is present also when you are doing right?" I asked him, "Have you ever thought of doing something for God, as a grown man—something of which He would approve? Or have you thought of God only as Someone to run to when you get into trouble? Have you ever thought of the fact that God has endowed you with certain splendid gifts that He expects you to use for Him and for your fellow-men? Have you ever wondered why at one moment you are inordinately proud of yourself and the next moment you feel overwhelmed with humiliation? As you come to be concerned less with yourself and your own feelings and more interested in fulfilling the purposes for which God gave you life you will gain freedom from these impulses to act and think childishly.

"You come to me," I continued, "suffering from feelings of self-depreciation, inferiority, and the like, and all of these have been in comparison with other people. You have had a good deal of pride in your acting and this is also in comparison with other people. Either you abase yourself or exalt yourself always in comparison with somebody else. I don't believe that you have once measured yourself by God's standards."

"What do you mean by God's standards?" he asked, "and how can I judge my acting by them?"

"Well, you compare your work with that of another actor whom you mentally select for the purpose and I rather guess that you do not suffer in the comparison. But that is not the basis of God's judgment of you. He rates you according to the measure in which you utilize the powers that He has given you—not according to what you are or will be, but by what you might be. St. Paul has some incisive observations on this subject. He says[5]:

> "If anyone imagines he is somebody he is deceiving himself, for he is nobody: let every one bring his own work to the test—then he will have something to boast about on his own account and not in comparison with his fellows."

"That sounds as if it had been written just for me," he answered, "but what happens if I submit to this test?"

"You will not come off with flying colors," I said. "I think you will be much humbler. You will surrender your false and childish pride; for wherever there is pride, there is or will be humiliation. Remember that when one has humbled himself before God he does not need any longer to be abased in the presence of his fellow-men. He no longer needs to carry a false front. He is honest with himself and his fellow-men because he has been honest with God. He becomes a perfectly normal man untroubled by either pride or abasement, conceit or inferiority."

"As you have been talking," he said, "the situation has definitely clarified. For the first time I am beginning to understand myself. If you will show me how to do it, I would like to submit to God's judgment."

"In that case, I suggest that we kneel in prayer and that you tell this to God."

He prayed: "God, I thank You for enabling me to come to

[5] Galatians VI:3 and 4.

You now not as a boy but as a grown-up man. I have never before talked to You as a man. Perhaps I haven't spoken to anybody as a man. I want to be honest with You. I have never truly been honest before. Deliver me from childish pride and discouragement. When I no longer think of You in childish ways I shall not behave childishly to people. I want to do something for Your glory, God. In the past I have done everything for my own. Help me in my acting to use the gifts You have given me so that I may become a better actor and a better man. . . ."

As he said good-bye to me, there was a subtle difference in his bearing that was notably lacking in his first approach; a grown-up-ness and a look of peace and quiet confidence which is possessed only by those "whose minds are stayed on God."

A few weeks after his final visit he wrote me a glowing letter in which the following paragraph occurs:

> "The interviews have meant more to me than I can ever tell. My life is altogether different and I am sure that it will continue to be so. No longer am I up in the clouds one minute and down in the cellar the next. I have found that by being keenly alert and ever watchful it is easy to reject childish and negative thoughts. Each victory thrills one and gives the right feeling of self-control and dominion. 'Thanks be to God, which giveth us the victory through our Lord Jesus Christ.' "

In response to an enquiry from me he wrote six months later declaring that never had things gone better with him in his home or in his work and that he had not experienced even a trace of the old symptoms. He added: "Now that I have become a man I have put away childish things." He said that when my letter came it had been necessary for him to think for a moment in order to realize what my questions meant, so far had he progressed. His faith has steadily increased and deepened. I believe that he has passed entirely beyond the reach of those feelings that had so profoundly disturbed his life.

The feeling of humiliation or inferiority is a widespread

disorder. It is an emotion that manifests itself in people who regard themselves as lacking in qualities and abilities possessed by the mass of mankind. It oftentimes has its beginning in childhood. It may be due to a physical, mental, social, or racial fact, that need not be but actually is made a handicap. A child who has some physical or organic defect, such as lameness, a cast in the eye, facial disfigurement, a birthmark, a cleft palate, a scar from chicken pox or from an accident, or one who is unduly short or tall, excessively fat or thin, is generally a subject of ridicule on the part of his schoolmates. Children are often very cruel to each other and many serious inferiorities are implanted in childhood minds on the school playground, especially when the games of the children are not supervised. Oftentimes in the farmyard it is observed that if one fowl sustains an injury, all the rest of the flock peck at the injured one and sometimes will kill it. A strain of this animal instinct seems to have remained in children, especially when they come together in a group.

Children are much more sensitive than adults to the impressions that they make upon others. A child may be permanently injured by thoughtless remarks, ridicule, or teasing. Parents will sometimes call their child an "ugly duckling" or in the presence of a boy say that they had wanted a girl, or in the presence of a girl say they had wanted a boy. It is cruel to tell a child that he is "stupid," "ugly," or "no good." Even a small child notices when a nickname that a parent gives him is said with a smile.

A feeling of inadequacy or humiliation in a child is often evidenced by stammering. Speech difficulty is a symptom of social maladjustment. It indicates that in other areas of life the child is having a difficult time to find its place and to meet competition. The frustration he has met with in life is reflected in his speech.

One of the most frequent causes of self-abasement in adults is wrong training which they received from their parents as children. An illustration of this comes to my mind.

I received a letter from a business man of my acquaintance who had made a marked success in the financial world. He invited me to dinner in his home in order that I might meet his son, twenty years of age, who was in serious difficulty. I accepted his invitation.

After dinner was over, according to the prearranged plan of the father and mother, the parents withdrew, leaving me alone with their son, Victor. As they were leaving the room, I noticed that the boy darted an angry glance towards them and one of irritation towards me.

When the door had been closed, I turned to him and said:

"Vic, I suppose you know that this dinner is a put-up job. Your parents arranged that they should clear out of the room so that you and I would be left alone because they felt you ought to talk to me about some of your problems. Now, I wish you might feel at ease, for I myself am not at all anxious to talk with you about yourself. I didn't ask for this interview. You don't have to say a word to me about yourself unless you wish to. We can talk about other things of interest and neither your father nor your mother will be any the wiser. Everything that passes in this room is in confidence, anyway."

Although Victor's face had been turned away while I was giving this explanation, I thought I detected the trace of a smile. He looked up and said:

"From the commencement of dinner I thought Dad had something up his sleeve and I think that you are awfully decent about it."

"Well, Vic," I replied, "while you certainly don't have to talk about yourself, after all we are here alone, and if there is anything that you would like to say, just go ahead and say it. It may help you to talk things out with somebody. I haven't discussed your affairs with your father."

"I am in a pretty bad jam," said Victor, "and Dad is terribly sore at me. You see he started from scratch himself and he counted on my making as great a success as he has, and because I haven't he has lost faith in me."

"Tell me the thing that has brought this trouble to a head," I suggested to him.

"Well, to make a long story short, I have lost my job. Jobs

are not easy to get nowadays, but through Father's influence I got one with a trust company. I was getting along very well except for the fact that the manager of the office seemed to have taken a scunner at me from the time I started to work. He has put several of his friends in positions in the office and didn't like the fact that I did my work better than they."

"You feel, then, that there was nothing wrong about your work?" I asked him.

"I certainly do," replied Victor. "I think I have done a better job at the teller's window and on the books than any of the fellows in the office. I won't play second fiddle to anybody."

"How do you account for the fact that you have been discharged?" I enquired.

"I will tell you what happened," he said. "I had made plans to celebrate the Thanksgiving holiday with some of my friends and bought a supply of liquor. I took a bottle of whisky down to the trust company with me and put it in my locker. I treated some of the boys and I guess I had been tippling a good deal during the day. Anyway, I got pretty well over the bay and before we closed for the day I went into the office of the manager and gave him a piece of my mind. I told him that he had been finding a soft place in the company for his friends; that he had used me rotten all the way through and I didn't propose to stand for it. I don't know what else I did, but some of the boys intervened and that night I got a telegram from the manager telling me that I had been discharged."

"What did your father say about that?" I asked Victor.

"Oh, he stormed around as usual and said that I had proved once again that I am a failure. 'You never succeed at anything,' he said. 'I get you a good job and you lose it. You will be a long while getting another like it. The manager of the trust company told me that he couldn't give you a recommendation.' So you see I am in a pretty bad fix."

"Well, so far, Victor, you have told me only about how well you have done your work at the office. I should judge that you are pretty confident of your ability. You have had other jobs before this one, haven't you?"

"Yes-s-s," he said, hesitatingly.

"Did you quit them of your own free will or were you discharged?" I asked him.

"In most cases I lost the job, but not because I wasn't able to do the work. I could do it as well as anybody else could, but my superiors seemed to pick on me."

"It looks to me," I said, "as if you are having a lot of trouble with people. Would you mind telling me how you explain this?"

"Oh, I don't know," he replied. "I don't seem to get along with men. I like women better. They are much more considerate and easier to get along with. I have a lot of women friends. I know perfectly well that you don't approve of my conduct—but I certainly seem to attract women."

"Tell me about it," I said. "I am interested in this aspect of your life, not just from idle curiosity, but because by my understanding better what is happening in some other areas, I may be able to help you more."

"To be frank with you," he responded, "I have always found women 'easy.' They are all that way if you know how to handle them. I think a young man ought to have some experiences like that and I have had plenty of them."

"Why do you say they are all like that?" I asked him.

"That is true of all that I have met, anyway. I meet them in funny ways sometimes. Some of them are married and some of them are single, but it makes no difference to me and it seems to make no difference to them. For instance, the other day I was walking with a young fellow along Fifth Avenue. As I was crossing one of the intersections a beautiful big car almost hit me, although I had the right of way. It was driven by a woman. I turned to her and said, 'You had better take some lessons in driving, hadn't you?' She didn't get sore, but simply smiled and said, 'Perhaps you will give me some.' Then I noticed she was a good looker. I said, 'When would you like to have them?' 'Right now is O.K. for me,' she said. So I said good-bye to my friend and spent the rest of the afternoon with her. She paid all the bills. She told me she was married. I have experiences like that all the time. I think every fellow is entitled to his fun and he certainly ought to be able to prove his manhood."

"You wouldn't try to prove a thing unless you had your doubts about it, would you?" I observed.

There was silence.

I realized that here was an individual for whom illicit sex relations had become an end in life. He discovered that no sooner had this become the compelling urge of his being than all the base things of the world began to minister to him. His desires were driven by one impulse and that impulse created a vacuum which drew into itself everybody and everything that catered to his passions. From his own limited experiences in regard to women, he generalized about the rest of womankind.

I said to Victor, "I am glad you gave me these confidences, but I think you are mistaken about women and maybe about yourself. What you have said is *a* truth, but you would be nearer *the* truth if you said that the kind of women who are attracted to you are the kind that get their way with you and not your way with them. Is that the way you prove your manhood?"

Again there was no answer.

I then asked him if there was any one thing that he could remember about his boyhood. He replied:

"I recall that when I was about four years old I was playing with a little express wagon in the street. One day two older boys slapped me, took the wagon away from me, and ran down the street with it. I went home crying and told mother what had happened."

"What did your mother say?" I enquired.

"She said, 'It is all right, darling. I will buy you a new wagon tomorrow and a better one. Don't cry now; you will get another and I will give you your first ride in it.'"

"But don't you think you could have got the wagon back if you had really wanted to?"

"Yes," he replied, "I suppose I could have, but I felt that a new one would be nicer than the old one."

"Victor, I'd like to draw something to your attention. You

tell me first of an auto and then of a wagon. In which one are you not a little boy? Are you a man in either one? I don't believe it!

"In all cases it's a woman who provides the car or the pocketbook. If you were talking with a psycho-analyst he would draw your attention to the fact that these women are substitutes for your own mother. Freud has some pertinent remarks on this point in his observations on the Oedipus complex. Now, isn't it true, Victor, that you are still the little boy who chases after motherly affections? And don't you love it when these women say to you 'dear boy' or 'you poor boy'?"

Once again there was silence.

The other early memories he related were similar to the one just described. His parents were always stepping in to solve his problems for him. If his mother tried to discipline him, his father intervened; and if his father commanded him to do anything, his mother would countermand the order. He had never been taught as a child how to look after himself or how to stand upon his own feet. After he had grown up, he still felt that people should all wait on him, that he was entitled to the attention and services of everyone. The world owed him a living, he believed.

It was necessary for me to terminate the interview at this point, but Victor asked for another appointment.

In the meantime I had a long talk with his parents. They confirmed his boyhood recollections. His father said to me:

"I had a tough time myself as a boy and Vic is my only son. I didn't want him to go through the things I had to endure."

"I think it might have been better for Vic," I said, "if his way had been more difficult. I am afraid the training you have given him has broken down his self-confidence, his belief in his own powers of achievement. That is one of the reasons why he has never been able to accomplish very much."

"In that case," said the father, "I guess I have been too hard on the boy. If I have helped to make him what he is, it is as much my fault as his."

From the mother I learned many additional details about

Victor's boyhood. His parents purchased for him a lot of jig-saw puzzles when that craze was in fashion. He spent hours of his time seated on the floor of the living room, playing with these puzzles. Both parents, and particularly the mother, in-stead of encouraging him to complete a puzzle on his own initiative and then praising his achievement rather than him-self, would invariably step in and assist Victor every time he met with any difficulty. She had done that even when he was playing with blocks as a tiny child. When friends came in and she was busy entertaining them, Victor discovered that by sulking or crying or developing a temper tantrum he could get his mother's attention and she would hurry to assist him. He had developed a behaviour formula something like this:

"I can never do anything myself.
I shall always need help.
If I make a fuss, somebody, usually a woman, will come along and do the thing for me.
I am entitled to have people wait on me."

It was easy to see why he liked women. They flattered him and, as he was good-looking, they were pleased with his atten-tions and told him so. They waited on him hand and foot. He met with a different reception in the business world. There he had to do things for himself for the first time in his life. Somebody was not always waiting to step in and solve his problems for him. So he became irritable with his superiors. He resented any criticism, no matter how constructive. He found it almost impossible to control his temper when he was reprimanded.

At the commencement of my next interview with Victor I said to him:

"Just as we were finishing our last talk, you were telling me about your success with women. I am interested to know whether or not you really enjoy your sex relations with them. Would you mind telling me this?"

He said: "In some ways I cannot say that I do, but some-how I seem to need them. Wherever I go on buses or subways or trains, I am always keeping an eye open for a girl. I guess I am built that way. I can't get along without them."

I explained to Victor what I had read in Dr. Karen Horney's book, *The Neurotic Personality of our Time:*[6]

> A great deal of sexual activity today is more an outlet for psychic tension than a genuine sexual drive and is therefore to be regarded more as a sedative than genuine sexual enjoyment or happiness. . . . An individual who needs sexuality as an outlet for the sake of allaying anxiety will be particularly incapable of enduring any abstinence, even of short duration. . . .

"Is that the reason, Vic," I said, "why you seem to need women and why you are upset when you are away from them for a while?"

"I have been wondering about that myself. I had supposed it was because I got along so much better with them. I seem to be happier with them. They are kinder and more attentive to me than men."

"Now, Vic," I said, "I have some plain unvarnished things to say to you. You are in your present mess because you have never really understood yourself. All your childhood memories and the additional information I have received from your parents shows that you believe the world owes you a living. Things were made so easy for you in your childhood that you want them made easy for you all the rest of your life. You have told me that you need the solace of your women friends, especially when you run into any difficulty. Because you can't stand up to life like a man, you want the soft comfort of a woman who flatters you. If you want to know why you have always failed in the past, I'd say it is because you have always played the part of a boy and never taken your place as a man."

"I don't see that that has got anything to do with my office work," Victor answered, a bit hotly. "What I do in my private life is none of the business of my boss or anybody else."

"The simple truth, Vic, is that what you do in your private

[6] Pp. 158-159.

life is reflected in, and is a part of, your business life. The two cannot be separated because you cannot divide your own life into water-tight compartments. You can't say, 'Over here is business and over there is my private life and they are not related one to the other.' The fact is they are both parts of one continuous whole. Each affects the other."

Victor sighed deeply.

"I wonder if you are really happy about the way things are going?" I asked him.

"I certainly am not," he said, somewhat shamefacedly, "and I will be glad if you can help me to put things right, but I don't see why we have to bring all these things up."

"We're working at a bigger job than you realize," I said to him. "I have something else to bring up right now. The putting right has to be done in your inner life. Have you ever thought of asking God's help?"

"No," he said. "Anyway, I haven't got any use for churches or ministers or priests. I really despise them. Of course," he added, graciously, "you are rather an exception."

"And you are sure you haven't projected some of your dislike of yourself on to churches and ministers and priests?" I asked. "Are you sure that it isn't yourself you despise?"

He dropped his head for a moment and then said:

"I guess you have got me there. I am sick and disgusted with myself. I said a moment ago I would like to put things right and I meant every word of it."

"You realize, of course, that I am not a psychiatrist. I am a minister. My business is to bring people into contact with God. The first necessity is for you to get right with Him. You wouldn't have come to me after your dislike of churches and ministers if you weren't really expecting help from God. It makes little difference if you were aware of that or not. It's true, isn't it, that your behaviour pattern is staying as a boy and not developing in your social, business, and spiritual life?"

He nodded assent.

"If you will take my guidance, I suggest for you to begin to act as a grown man towards God and then you will establish a

new pattern of social and business relations on the basis of
maturity.'"

"I see what you mean, but how can I make a beginning?" he
asked.

"By asking God not to solve your problems for you, but so to
transform you that you will have the necessary strength within
you to solve your own problems. You have bluffed your way
for a long time. You fooled yourself very successfully and
thought that you were fooling others, but every time they called
your bluff. You must be honest with yourself, with your fellow-
men, and with God."

"I think I have got that far," he said. "I have been bluffing.
I have even been trying to bluff God, but I am ready now to
admit that I have been a failure. I am even ready to surrender
my private life to God—every bit of it. I am ready to do whatever He wants me to."

"What about the companionships that belong to your old
life?" I enquired.

"I will break them off," he replied. "With your encouragement and strength from God I can do it."

"Here's a verse from the New Testament I want to give you.
Please repeat it after me:

"I can do all things through Christ who strengtheneth me."[7]
He repeated it.

"Now," I asked, "are you ready to go ahead?"

"Yes," he replied, "I am ready to see this thing through. I
don't know why it is that sometimes I feel proud of myself and
sometimes I am down in the dumps. When I am with my
women friends, I think I am a wonderful fellow; my bosses
always made me feel as if I was no good and I was humiliated
when they gave me the sack. Now I come to you and feel that
you have seen through me from the beginning and yet you
don't throw me out. You know the worst about me, but while
I am ashamed of my past, somehow I don't feel humiliated."

"That's exactly what I have been waiting for you to come to.

[7] Philippians IV:13. (Revised Version.)

You are ready now for God to deal with you. You are truly contrite now."

I suggested that we should kneel in prayer.

"You pray first," I said.

For a long time there was silence, and then Victor broke down completely. His whole body was shaken with sobs. When he had steadied himself, he said:

"God, I need to get strength from You. It is the first time I have ever really asked it. I have been a bluffer and a braggart, but I am ready to admit it all now. I am ashamed and sorry for my past. Somehow I couldn't seem to do anything else, but with Your strength I can do better. Help me to change my life so that mother and dad may be proud of me. I have brought enough sorrow to them. God, I surrender completely. I hold nothing back. Take me and bless me and help me."

When Victor had finished his prayer, I thanked God for what he had done for the boy and for the new life that was opening out before him. When I prayed for Victor's mother and father, the boy broke down again.

When the interview was concluded, I found that we had been talking for three hours. I had at least eight or ten additional interviews of shorter duration with Victor.

For the first two or three months it was a hard battle for him because a lot of his women friends were writing and telephoning him despite the fact that he had told them he was through with his old life. He told me that the one passage of Scripture especially helpful to him on many trying occasions was, "I can do all things through Christ who strengtheneth me." In hours when he was almost overwhelmed by temptation, Victor said that if he were able even for a moment to close his eyes and say to himself, "I can do all things through Christ who strengtheneth me," the sense of Christ's presence became so real that the force of the temptation was broken.

Every month that has passed has seen an advance in Victor's spiritual development. His faith in God has steadily increased. His character has developed to the extent that now he is no longer dependent either in his religious attitudes nor in his rela tionships to his friends and business associates. At last he has gained the victory over both humiliation and its accompaniment of unreasonable pride, which together had almost wrecked his life.

Any individual who is suffering from a sense of humiliation or inferiority is a very difficult person with whom either to live or to work. He is especially exacting with those who are close to him in life. He is constantly finding fault with the members of his family and with his fellow employees and superiors. If he is a parent, he will frequently have one of the children on the carpet lecturing and haranguing the child for as long as half an hour. He is the last to recognize where the trouble lies—that it is not in the child, but in the father. There is implanted in him such a deep feeling of inadequacy and imperfection that he desires to see in the loved ones in his home the perfection that he himself lacks. Therefore he becomes unreasonably angry at any deviation from the kind of conduct which he thinks ought to be observed.

Conversely, whenever one sees people aggressive, domineering, quarrelsome, it is generally an evidence of the existence of some inferiority, either actual and outward or inwardly subjective. When one meets with an individual who is overbearing, restless, and making exacting and unreasonable demands on others, with a temper that breaks forth every now and then in some excess, one can be perfectly sure that there is a deep-rooted feeling of humiliation present in the episode. He is suffering from self-debasement.

In early life such an individual usually bluffs and brags. It is a psychological and spiritual fact that our brags express our fears. We do not boast about what we know to be genuine achievements. It is only in the areas of life about which we feel inadequate that we resort to camouflage and deception.

The kind of man who is a tyrant in his own home, in social life is usually intolerant of the opinions of others. He asserts his views with tremendous emphasis and by the weight of ridicule or argument endeavours to sweep away all opposition to his ideas. He seeks to build up his own pride by being critical of others. If he can only put them down, he will rise in his own estimation. He has really lost confidence in himself. He is almost overwhelmed at times by a feeling of humiliation.

Maimonides, a noted Jewish rabbi who lived in the twelfth century says, "Humility is the mean between arrogance and self-abasement." That golden mean is found in the Christian ideal of character.

Humility is not something that can be forced upon the individual from without. It must arise from within. Nor can we compel ourselves to be humble if we do not possess genuine humility. We may wear the vestments of humility; we may repeat certain stock phrases that indicate self-effacement; we may play a part like an actor on the stage, but ultimately we shall deceive no one but ourselves. True humility involves an awareness of one's achievements and one's failures, one's strength and one's weakness, one's capacities and one's limitations. True humility prevents our attempting what lies beyond our power and our neglecting those tasks that are within our capacity. Through it all we shall feel neither superior nor inferior.

Kahlil Gibran in *Sand and Foam* makes a profound observation on this point:

Only those beneath me can envy or hate me.
I have never been envied nor hated; I am above no one.
Only those above me can praise or belittle me.
I have never been praised nor belittled; I am below no one.

Here is a high standard indeed. The man who achieves it never experiences humiliation or pride. I know of no other way by which this ideal is reached than by surrendering one's estimate of oneself and being willing to accept the judgment of God. Thereafter one will not feel either humiliation or pride in the presence of men.

VII. "*Train up a Child . . .* "

"Train up a child in the way he should go: and when he is old, he will not depart from it."

—Proverbs XXII:6

"Do not sin against the child."

—Genesis XLII:22

"Suffer little children, and forbid them not, to come unto me; for of such is the kingdom of heaven.

—St. Matthew XIX:14

"Whoso shall receive one such little child in my name receiveth me."

—St. Matthew XVIII:5

"Withhold not correction from the child."

—Proverbs XXIII:13

". . . a child left to himself bringeth his mother to shame."

—Proverbs XXIX:15

". . . from a child thou hast known the holy scriptures, which are able to make thee wise unto salvation through faith which is in Christ Jesus."

—II Timothy III:15

"Except ye be converted, and become as little children, ye shall not enter into the kingdom of heaven."

—St. Matthew XVIII:3

"When I was a child, I spake as a child, I understood as a child, I thought as a child; but when I became a man, I put away childish things."

—I Corinthians XIII:11

". . . and a little child shall lead them."

—Isaiah XI:6

"And, ye fathers, provoke not your children to wrath: but bring them up in the nurture and admonition of the Lord."

—Ephesians VI:4

I LOOKED at the woman who sat across the desk from me and noted the lines of care on her face. Her mannerisms revealed the tension that gripped her. Unceasingly she folded and unfolded her gloves, the while moving uneasily in her chair.

"My trouble," she said, "is with my son. He is a terrible problem. I have tried everything I could think of in dealing with him, without result. He is ten times more difficult to manage than our two girls. I am really at my wit's end to know what to do with him."

I gleaned the following information from her regarding her son.

Harold was ten years of age, physically well built but "high strung and nervous." At school he was inattentive, troublesome, and given to silly behaviour. He was constantly tripping other boys at recess or else poking them with his elbow. He had been reported time and again to the principal for fighting—usually with boys who were younger and smaller than he. He ranked low in class standing, generally with the last five or ten in the room.

At home, where he had two sisters, one aged eight and the other seven, he was constantly in trouble. From early morning until bedtime he quarrelled with his younger sister. He could not pass her at any time without taunting, slapping, or tripping her. This treatment had made her exceedingly nervous and irritable. She was always even-tempered, however, until her brother appeared on the scene. He was perpetually trying to foment a quarrel between the older sister and the younger. Always he kept telling them that they were "saps," "dames," "ninnies." He never ceased boasting to them of his achievements, talking usually in a loud and high-pitched voice and assuring them that girls could never be anything else but "dumb." He had no hobbies and played very little with other boys.

His mother could not recall a single undertaking that he had finally completed. After an hour or two he would tire of work or play and lose all interest in it. Every game with his sisters ended in a battle, with both girls crying and claiming that he had cheated. The older girl, aged eight, had overtaken him at school and this was a constant source of irritation to them both.

The boy's father was a young medical man with an unusually large practice. The boy saw very little of his father even at mealtime, as the doctor was in very great demand. When they did meet the father usually upbraided his son for not making a better showing at school.

In response to my question as to how the parents had sought to deal with the boy the mother answered:

"Well, we have tried for a couple of years to break down his intolerable sense of superiority. Whenever we have found him lording it over his sisters and boasting of his achievements, we pointed out his poor showing at school and told him that he had nothing to brag about. His father has had to strap him several times for the way in which he has treated his little sister Alice."

Interrupting at this point a copious outburst of tears I suggested to her that some major adjustments would have to be made in the home before her son could be expected to develop a normal mode of life.

"It looks to me," I said to her, "as if you and your husband could do much better with your boy if you would drop most of your previous ways of managing your children. Take an inventory of what you have accomplished and make a fresh start with the idea of insuring better results. I will help you after I get acquainted with Harold."

The following day she brought her son to see me after school and left him in my study. When I came in, I found him peering into a microscope that was standing on a table. He looked up quickly and said, "Is this yours?"

"Yes, Harold," I replied, "that is mine."

"I would like to have one of these things," he said.

"Why? What would you do with it?" I asked.

"I would like to make a great discovery about germs and become famous," he replied.

"Why do you want to be famous?" I asked him.

"Well," was the reply, "it is nice to have everybody taking notice of you and your name in the papers so that people will read about you. Then I am sure mother and dad would be proud of me."

"I am sure they are proud of you, now, Harold," I said. He gave me a sour look and I knew he did not see the truth of my statement.

"What would you like to be when you are a man?" I enquired.

"I would like to be a great doctor or an explorer. Explorers are famous, aren't they? Everybody reads about them."

"Yes, Harold," I answered, "that is true; but do you realize how hard they had to work before they could make great discoveries? One doesn't become famous just by working for fame alone. A man becomes famous as a result of his having worked hard to get good results in whatever job he has been given. No matter how simple and humble his work may appear to be, he gives his best to it. Fame comes to people because of success in achievement or because of benefiting mankind. Do you see where this differs from your idea, Harold?"

"Yes, sir, I do," he replied, "but I didn't realize that that was the way people became famous."

"I am glad you understand what I mean," I said to him. "Now that you want to be a success in life, what are you doing towards achieving it? What plans are you making? Have you got a goal? Is there still more that you could do if you settled right down to business?"

"I am afraid I haven't been doing everything I could," Harold replied. "I haven't liked my school work and my marks have been poor."

"Well, Harold," I said, "that is the very place where real effort can be made. It is only as you do your daily work well that you can hope for success in later life. You say that you haven't been getting good marks at school. I wonder why. You look to me like a bright boy. What is it that is preventing you from making good marks? There must be something. Wouldn't you like to get these obstacles moved from your path? Perhaps you need somebody to help you. Suppose we try to work this thing out together."

"I wish you would help me," Harold replied, earnestly. "I really want to do better."

"What is it that discourages you most," I enquired, "your home or your school?"

"Both of them, I guess," Harold said. "I am afraid I will never get on well in school because dad says that I am dull, and I don't get on well at home, either. There is nobody but girls there and they play only sissy games. Dad is so busy that he is seldom home at all and the girls are always taking my things, especially Alice. I don't like her. Girls are dumb, anyway."

As Harold talked, his voice rose higher and higher and he swaggered round the room. He had a slight stammer which was more marked when he became excited.

"Sit down for a few minutes, Harold," I suggested, "and we will talk some more about this. Tell me what happens at home when things go bad with you."

"Oh, mother and dad get cross at me," he replied, "and I guess I deserve it because I lose my temper with the girls."

Then looking up quickly with a pleading expression in his eyes, he said:

"I wish you would tell me, sir, how I can control myself better. I get discouraged at school and then I go home cross and strike and shove my sisters and talk back to mother. Then mother gets cross at me and that just makes things worse. As soon as I say nasty things to them I am sorry for it, but I can't bring myself to tell them so and then I am sent off to my room. Sometimes I have a quarrel at home before I go to school. Then I am cranky when I get there and I do something that makes the teacher cross at me."

"Well, Harold," I said, "you and I will try to get to the bottom of this thing and see what it is that gets you all out of sorts. By the way, you have a good memory, haven't you? What is the earliest thing that you can recall about the days when you were a small boy?"

Without a moment's hesitation, he answered:

"I remember being lost one time. My father took me to the hospital one time and left me in the car. He was away for a long time. I got lonesome and cried. Then I got out of the car and ran away so far that I got lost and I couldn't find my way back. Everybody was looking for me. They took me home in an ambulance and there were men with white coats who talked to me and gave me candy."

"What else do you remember?" I asked, encouragingly.

"I remember when the boy in the house next to us ran away. They didn't find him until after dark. His mother was crying. That was before I got lost."

"These things that you can remember from your early boyhood are very important," I said. "You say that you remember that your father left you for a long time and that you were lonesome and then you got lost. Isn't it true that sometimes you feel that you are still lost and that you often get very lonesome?"

"What made you say that?" Harold asked.

"Well, I have a kind of feeling, Harold," I replied, "that you think your parents don't care for you as much as they once did. These two memories tell me a lot about you. You were so impressed when the other boy's mother cried for him after he ran away that you wanted to test your mother's love by running away yourself." Harold looked fascinated. I continued, "Ever since, you have been doing one naughty thing after another to upset both your mother and father to get proof for yourself that you mean very very much to them both. Maybe I might tell you in confidence that I have seen your mother cry just about you." Harold was deeply moved—delighted that his mother had cried about him and yet welling up with tears that might have been both self-pity and a genuine sympathy with her suffering.

Then I continued: "Did you ever ask yourself why you dislike Alice, your little sister?"

"I don't know why, but I never did like her," he responded.

"I think I can tell you, Harold," I said. "When she was born you thought because your parents were so proud of her that they had ceased to love you—that your father had 'left' you for your baby sister, and that made you feel like running away. But I want you to notice, Harold, that when you got lost your mother and father left the two girls and went hunting all over the city for you. They were very anxious to find you because they love you and they have never loved you less because Alice was born. You have a very big place in their hearts. I know that because they have told me so. If you could only realize that your mother and father are very proud of you and love you dearly, you could be a great help to them at home. You see your father, although he is a young man, is a very busy doctor. He is away from home helping people a lot of the time. Often you are the only man in the house. Wouldn't it be nice if your two sisters could look up to you as their protector? You could be their hero if you want to. You said you wanted to make your mother and father proud of you. Well, this is one of the ways in which you can do it right now. While your father is busy at the hospital or visiting sick people, you could do some of the things at home that he does when he is there."

"I never thought I could start to be successful right at home, but I see what you mean," Harold responded. "I would like to do that."

"I believe you can, Harold," I said.

"I am sure I can," he replied.

"Now, there is something else I would like you to talk about and it is very important. Harold, I notice you have been attending Sunday school and church regularly. You have learned about God. Have you ever asked Him to help you with your difficulties?"

He answered, very quietly: "Yes, I have prayed about it over and over again, but it just doesn't seem to do any good. I guess God is busy like father is."

Tears were in the boy's eyes.

"There is no need for you to be discouraged, Harold," I said. "Boys are not the only people who have difficulty in finding that their prayers do good. The trouble usually is that we ask God for things, and when He answers our prayers we don't realize He is giving us what we asked for because He doesn't do it in just the way we expect. I am sure you can help God to answer your prayers by working with Him to bring the answer. Have you ever thought that God is planning for you and loving you just as your father is even though you are not aware of it?"

Harold said nothing, but I knew that he understood me.

"Do you remember reading in Sunday school how Jesus visited a man whose name was Zacchæus who lived in Jericho and everybody hated him?" I asked. "He was a tax-gatherer for the Romans. The Jews despised him and they showed by their manner that they didn't like him, and then he became more hateful to them until no one in the city would have anything to do with him. Perhaps you remember that Jesus visited this man and had dinner with him. And the Master said to Zacchæus, 'I am come to seek and to save that which is lost.' You see Zacchæus missed a turning in the road and lost his way in life. Jesus showed him the way back to the right pathway."

"I remember that story," said Harold. "After Jesus had talked to Zacchæus, the tax-gatherer told Him he was going to try to make up for all the bad things he had done and wherever he had taken money from people he was going to give them back four times as much. We had that lesson a few weeks ago in Sunday school."

"That is fine, Harold," I said. "I thought you would know the story. Well, I want you to think about those words of Jesus, 'I am come to seek and to save that which is lost.' You told me that when you were a boy you got lost, and I asked you if you didn't feel sometimes that you were still lost. You see you too have missed the road, but Jesus says that He will show you the right path and He is using me today to help you find your way back. When you thought that your parents didn't love you, you were losing your way and then when you quarrelled with your sisters and annoyed your mother, you were straying farther away.

"Don't you think it would be a good idea, Harold," I continued, "if you and I should kneel down now side by side and you should ask God to guide you back to the road that will lead you to happiness and success and that will make you a better boy both at home and in school?"

Harold agreed and in a simple petition for help he said:

"Oh, God, help me to find my way and be a better boy at school and with mother, dad and the girls. Help me to make them proud of me, for Jesus' sake. Amen."

Then I thanked God aloud for having heard Harold's prayer and for the new beginning the boy had made in that moment.

When we had risen from our knees, Harold said:

"I feel better already. Can I come back and see you again?"

"You certainly can, Harold," I said. "I shall be very happy to see you. Suppose we make a date for tomorrow afternoon."

Before Harold left on the day of the first interview, I said:

"Would you mind if I talk this matter over with your father and mother and tell them about the new beginning you have made? Maybe they would like to make a new beginning, too, along with you."

"Yes, sir," he said, his eyes sparkling, "that would be great, but," he added as tears came, "they won't change any—it won't help at all."

"I am sure that it will help them, Harold, just as much as it will help you," I assured him.

A few minutes before the time that his mother was to return, I suggested to Harold that he go into the washroom and scrub away the evidence of the tears on his face, for he had cried also at the end of his prayer.

The next step was a long interview with the father and mother. I told them that Harold was suffering from loneliness, discouragement, and a craving for appreciation that was almost insatiable.

"But," interrupted the mother, "he is dreadfully superior to everybody."

I explained to her that the boy's fighting and swaggering was accounted for by his desperate efforts to gain a place for himself in family life because he thought that Alice and her older sister had taken his place.

"He is trying to attract your attention," I said, "even though he has to make himself a nuisance in order to do this. His superiority is only apparent. It is not real. It is over-compensation for the deadening sense of being left without affection or attention. He feels that even God has no interest in him."

I pointed out the significant fact that Harold was the oldest child in the home. Two years later a girl was born. When Harold was ten years of age he was overtaken in school by his sister, Helen, the middle child. She was an unusually bright girl and had a natural aptitude for study.

I drew the parents' attention also to the fact that they had been in the habit of praising every achievement that Helen had made and contrasting her cleverness with a backwardness of the boy.

"Here is something," I said to them, "that you should have no difficulty in correcting. You must learn to give more encouragement to Harold. There shouldn't be direct competition between your children. It will build up antagonisms that may last for years. Every time you have drawn Harold's attention to his failure, you have deepened his feeling of loneliness and discouragement. He has been compelled to resort to cheating and fighting to gain his point and to make an impression on others. Your boy has been striving for a little appreciation."

"But why should Harold be so lonely?" his mother asked. "We have tried to give him everything that he needed and there are always people round him at home."

"The trouble has been," I said, "that Harold has felt that you haven't given him the one thing he wants—affection and love. You see you didn't prepare his mind for the arrival of his baby sisters. Just think for a moment of what a blow their coming was to this sensitive boy of yours. He had been the centre of the home and the object of unceasing attention. Then suddenly he found himself thrust aside and apparently neglected. Two usurpers came and sat themselves upon his throne. All homage was now paid to them."

"But," interrupted his mother, "he hasn't had any great dislike of Helen. His antagonism has seemed directed mainly to his younger sister, Alice."

"There is a very good reason for that," I answered. "When Helen was born, Harold was only two years of age and apparently he was unaware of any change in the home relationship but when a year and a half later Alice arrived, a little boy three and a half years old felt that his place had been taken by another. He hated his younger sister with all the intensity of his being. That is the reason why he has never missed an opportunity of slapping or tripping her. She has been his sworn enemy. He felt that Alice had robbed him of your affection and he couldn't forgive her for this fancied wrong."

I then spoke of how Dr. Alfred Adler, in his book, *Understanding Human Nature*,[1] tells of a little girl of the age of six who had become quite delicate and therefore was the centre of the home. At this time a baby sister was born. This was a terrible blow to the first child because she found herself pushed from the centre to the circumference of her parents' attention. One day the body of a little girl was found in a brook near the village where the six-year-old child lived. Later on another child was found in the same brook. A careful watch was kept. To the surprise of everybody the child, aged six, was caught just after having thrown a third baby girl into the water. She had no dislike for boys, but she saw her baby sister in these girls and, in destroying them, she felt that she was getting rid of her sister whom she blamed for the loss of her parents' attention and affection.

"If parents only knew how much damage can be done to the personality of an older child by the birth of a baby brother or sister, they would be at greater pains to prepare the older child for the advent of the younger one. The older child or children

[1] Garden City Publishing Company, Inc., Garden City, New York.

should be taught to regard their coming into the world and the coming of each new life as a gift of God and it should be considered a most important event in which all the family will participate. All should coöperate to make life pleasant for the newcomer, but above all, the older children should be assured that their place in the affection and interest of their parents will not be imperilled to the slightest degree by the fact that it will have to be shared by the new brother or sister," I said.

"There is another point," said Harold's mother, "which I should like to have cleared up. Why is Harold so contemptuous about girls in general? He seems to think that men and boys are superior kinds of creatures. He is always talking about 'dames,' 'sissies,' and 'ninnies.' Everything masculine is to him of a higher order."

"Well, I am sure you will admit," I said to her, "that Harold has been in the minority in the home. Haven't you usually sided with the two girls when there has been a quarrel? Harold's father is away all day and I gather from some things Harold told me in our conversations that when he comes home at night, tired after a busy day, he usually takes sides with you and the girls and scolds Harold for his misconduct. The situation could be saved if the boy were able to feel that his father would take the trouble at least to find out what was the thing in Harold that needed correction. If his father could discuss the boy's problems and difficulties, it would ease the tension in Harold's life. Occasionally I have met a grown-up man whose failure in love and marriage was traceable directly to the fact that he was an only boy in a family of girls. In every such instance the father is the key to the problem. He can help his boy to coöperate better with the rest of the family. A battleground where two or more girls are constantly warring with a boy is not a home.

"I have told you," I continued, "that your boy made a new beginning. I want you to understand what has happened so that you can help him achieve the goal he now has in mind."

Harold's mother and father were members of my church and attended its services with a fair degree of regularity. On a previous occasion, however, they had admitted that they did not take a personal interest in the religious experience of their children. His father had never heard Harold on even one occasion say his evening prayers. In earlier years his mother had listened to his prayers, but latterly had neglected this intimate contact with her son.

I pointed out to them both the urgent necessity for remedying this situation. I said:

"During his first interview in my study your boy committed his life to God and asked His help to do better at school and at home. Harold is going to have a difficult time unless both of you help him at this point. It is important especially that his father should take a deep interest in his religious development."

"I am very glad that you have brought these matters to our attention," the father interjected. "His mother and I will do our part. I am afraid that we have let the poor boy down pretty badly."

"If you are going to do your best for the boy, you must know more about Harold than I have told you," I said to the father. "I think that perhaps you would get a better perspective of his life as a whole if I should show you how definitely habit patterns have formed—not just in the last year or two but back in his early boyhood. You will see my point when I have told you of Harold's earliest memories. I have typed out for you the significant details of these memories."

I passed to each of Harold's parents a separate copy of the memories as outlined here.

(First Memory)

I remember being lost one time.
My father . . . left me.
He was away a long time.
I got lonesome and cried.
I got out . . . and ran away.
I got lost and I couldn't find my way back.
Everybody was looking for me. . . . They took me
  home . . . talked to me . . . gave me candy. . . .

(Second Memory)

I remember that the boy in the house next to us ran
'away.

His mother was crying.
That was before I got lost.

I drew the attention of Harold's parents to the first memory
and said, "Look at that second line, 'My father . . . left me.'
Of course you know and I know, Doctor, that when you left
him that time at the hospital you were visiting a patient, and
although you left him in the car, you had invited him to ride
with you so that you might have his companionship. Now
Harold really knows this, but he is not yet aware of his knowledge. He would be helped by your explaining to him that you
have a job that requires you to see patients when they need
you and to get your social life when you can. This will not
be news to Harold, but it will be healing balm to his feelings
of 'being left.'

"Another fact which he has not noticed and you haven't
explained to him is that you have been leaving not just him,
but the girls also.

"Note the third line in Harold's first memory—'He was
away a long time.' He has never forgotten the length of time
that you were away. He missed you so much because he loves
you. Suppose you tell him sometime soon it seemed to you, too,
that you had been a long time away from him and that you
missed him because you love him so much. I suggest this because Harold still feels that you 'leave him.'

"Now read on to the next line—'I got lonesome and cried.'
Isn't it probable that Harold is still lonesome but that, as he
has become older, he won't let the girls or you see him cry and
so you see that he gets cross and teases the girls instead? I
suspect that his quarrelsomeness is a screen to hide something
else. Couldn't you both arrange to meet Harold on his own
terms more often to keep him from being so lonely? Wouldn't
it be worth while to invite in some boy playmates in whom
Harold would be interested?

"You will see that the next line in his first memory reads,

'I got lost and I couldn't find my way back.' Harold is talking of an incident that happened years ago, but the boy is still lost and can't find his way back. You will both have to search for him even though he is right in the room with you. I think you know what I mean, don't you—that there is a part of Harold that you have never been able to reach. When the search has been successful there must be no doubt in Harold's mind that you have found him.

"In this legendary memory of his I see, 'Everybody was looking for me . . . they took me home.' Harold will know that you have found him now only if you understand that his various difficulties at home and in school are disguised forms of running away and that you, his parents, must go in search of him and bring him back yourselves.

"It is possible," I continued, "that Harold thinks of me as one of the 'men with white coats who talked' to him, even though I don't actually wear a white coat. May I suggest, Doctor, that you literally wear one of your white coats some day and sit down and talk to Harold at the hospital in man to man fashion so that he may have a feeling that he is your equal?"

"It never occurred to me," replied the father, "that Harold's early memories could be so definitely related to his present difficulties."

"That is a revelation to many people," I said, "but I am not through yet on this point. Both of you know your Bible sufficiently well to remember that there is a story in it about a boy who was lost. Harold remembers when he was found on that occasion long ago that candy was given to him. He took that as an indication that the searchers were glad that they had found him. In the Bible story about the lost boy we are told that he had no sooner come in sight of home than his father, not waiting for him to complete the journey, ran to meet him and fell on his neck and kissed him. I am sure that that boy had no doubt at all in his mind about the welcome he received from his father. I think that Harold now knows the road home. In fact, I can tell you that he is on his way home, but I am very desirous that when he gets there there will be no mistaking the warmth of the welcome he will receive. Mind you, this is not to exclude the girls. Your treatment of Harold must be of such a kind that he will want them in on it too."

At this point I noticed that Harold's mother, who had been deeply affected by the whole interview, was now crying softly. His father was blinking his eyes, trying desperately to keep back the tears.

"There is one thing more I want to mention now," I said to them. "It is on the second memory of Harold's concerning the neighbour boy who was lost. Harold specifically said that this happened before he ran away. You see Harold must have been looking for something that he himself had lost before he ran away. He has always remembered that the other boy's mother had cried. But I see now that it is not the other boy's mother who is crying, but Harold's mother. Harold has known that the other boys' mothers cry with sorrow when they are lost and from joy when they are found. It seems to me that both of you are ready now to welcome back the lost boy who is finding his way home. Isn't that true?"

Without waiting for an answer, I went into the study which adjoins the consulting-room and found Harold patiently waiting for me. He had come for an appointment without his parents knowing that I had sent for him.

I said, "Come into the consulting-room, Harold."

As he stepped over the threshold, his eyes widened with surprise. That his appearance was totally unexpected by his parents was evident from the look on their faces. Harold knew instantly that something had happened to his parents. They were different in a way that he couldn't explain. His mother really was crying and his father's reserve had been momentarily swept to the winds. Silently I stepped out of the room, closing the door behind me. Into my mind flashed a sentence spoken by a father in the long ago:

"This my son was dead, and is alive again; he was lost, and is found."[2]

Harold's father was even better than his word. No matter

[2] Luke xv:24.

how busy he was in his practice, he found time at least once or twice a week to spend an hour or two in the evening in his boy's bedroom, where Harold was the host and his father the guest. In this informal atmosphere they talked over the boy's interests and problems and his spiritual development. A bond of genuine comradeship has been formed between them. Week by week the doctor has discussed his son's religious ideas with him and the spiritual life of the father has been deepened and enriched by this fellowship.

Harold no longer feels lonely, neglected, ready to run away literally or figuratively; he feels that he "belongs" to the family as a whole, and to his school. Teachers could not account for his transformation. Harold told them simply that he got a different hunch about things. . . .

I notice that now, when Harold's mother comes in to see me, she no longer folds and unfolds her gloves, the while moving uneasily in her chair. . . .

Oliver Wendell Holmes has said that a child's education ought to be begun with his grandfather. While heredity is important, as Holmes suggests the child's environment is of even greater significance. One cannot make too early a beginning in either the secular or the spiritual training of the child. The wise man of Israel said:

"Train up a child in the way he should go: and when he is old, he will not depart from it."

Dr. Fritz Künkel, in his book, *Let's Be Normal,*[3] gives an impressive illustration of how early in the life of a child his behaviour pattern begins to form. He talks about a child less than three years old, to whom he gives the name "Carl Z." When the nurse that had been in charge of this child left the house permanently the boy became quite ill. He refused food. His sleep was fitful and broken. He lost weight and became pale and sickly. The child's condition was traced to the behaviour form of his nurse. She had suffered from inferiority, which was revealed in her belief that she was not efficient and

[3] Ives Washburn, Inc., publisher, New York.

that she would inevitably be discharged when the children she was caring for grew up. Her methods of dealing with the child led to a complete helplessness on his part, but to the parents it seemed a remarkable proof of her self-sacrifice and understanding. The boy ate only when she was present and went to sleep only if assured that she was in the adjoining room. Even when he was learning to walk she tried to spare him every failure, so that he became timid rather than brave. He dared not take a step unless the nurse's hands were by him. He would walk on an even floor, but he had never stepped over a threshold.

"Here," says Dr. Künkel, "is the principal defect in his character: *he has never learned to take the risk of failure.*"

On reaching the threshold he would yell for his nurse and she would lift him over it. Even in building a tower of blocks the nurse ensured that he would succeed in his efforts.

Dr. Künkel, in dealing with this case, had to explain the situation with the utmost clarity to the mother. She altered her mode of dealing with the boy. The final test came one day as the boy stood in front of the threshold between his room and his parents' bedroom, calling and crying.

"The mother did not move, but repeated to him in a friendly voice, 'Come along, my boy; you are big enough.' It took half an hour for the child to become quiet; another quarter of an hour elapsed while he stood silently in front of the threshold, raising his foot from time to time as if he were going to dare the adventure. The mother bent over her mending-basket for a moment, and when she raised her head the boy was standing in the middle of the room. The mother could have spoiled everything at this point by a clumsy remark. She noticed clearly the child's beaming expression and would have liked to break out in a song of triumph. But she knew that if she did that the child would demand a reward for his accomplishment, and so she found it more objective to accept the crossing of the threshold as something quite usual. She was right."

She succeeded, in a few months, in bringing the child to the point where he would remain alone in a room and climb and exercise by himself. His resistance to eating disappeared; his sleeping became quieter, and the most tenacious of all symptoms—the boy's anxiety—was gradually overcome. He ceased to worry about his own importance. He is now able to play with his young friends and is getting along splendidly in a kindergarten.

Everyone who has dealt with the psychological and spiritual problems of adults has met with grown-up men and women who were altogether incapacitated from making their way in life because of the destructive behaviour patterns they have formed in childhood. I have seen even husbands and wives utterly dependent upon a parent, and on the death of the parent utterly dependent on one or other of their children.

There are people who are spiritually, as well as secularly, dependent on others. There is a threshold of the spiritual life across which every child must be trained to step. When that step has been taken the boy or girl has entered upon an experience of religion that is his or her own, a knowledge of God and of spiritual reality that is first-hand and genuine.

One cannot begin too early in teaching a child about God. Even before the child reaches the age of understanding the parents may begin his training in the spiritual life by offering an audible prayer each night above the crib in which the child is lying. Simple Scripture passages may be stored away in the child's mind even before he begins to learn "Mother Goose" rhymes. Bedtime prayers afford a definite opportunity to influence the spiritual development of children. Impressions are so quickly planted in the fertile mind of a child that only a few of them are necessary to convince the child that either or both parents consider prayers to be important or worthless.

Adults often recall definite impressions existing as earliest memories about religion; that one or both parents were very sincere or insincere in their attitude to religion and that these impressions brought about part, if not the whole, of their adult spiritual activity or inactivity.

Children are liable to identify their own personalities with that of their parents, so that oftentimes they have no individuality of their own. If they are trained to pray and go through divine service only as their parents do, without participating in these services actively, they are merely identifying themselves with their parents and are having a second-hand religious experience. The goal for each parishioner is a spontaneous spiritual activity. Even as children learn first to read and write and to play games, so they are able to worship better when they are sure of parental approval; but this is only temporary. Just as no boy or girl will ever do well in school or at play, so, too, no child will do well in any spiritual activity who continually awaits parental approval or who does only what the parents like to do and in exactly the same way. Only as a child feels himself an individual separate from and yet in loving relationship to his parents, only as he feels confidence in himself and in them and a mutual sympathetic understanding is he free as an individual to commune directly with God.

The kind of religion that presents God to the mind of a child as an ever-present, sympathetic, understanding, all-powerful Friend and Protector will bear fruit in the development of moral and spiritual traits of character and will give to the child a feeling of security, peace and inner strength.

On one occasion a mother came to me for advice regarding her little girl, Rose, six years of age, who used to wake up night after night crying out in terror. She had been having these nightmares intermittently over a period of more than a year. We could not find any incident in earlier years that had caused them. Since the little girl was very intelligent and a regular attendant at Sunday school, I felt sure that religion could minister to her need.

One evening when I was having dinner with Rose's parents, I had a talk with the little girl. I said to her:

"Rose, I have some secrets to discuss with you."

Knowing that a child likes a touch of mystery, I whispered to her:

"What happens when you have a bad dream?"

"My mummy says I scream and hop out of bed and run down the hall," Rose answered, in a whisper.

"Your mummy says," I interrupted. "Don't *you* know what you do?"

"No," Rose replied, "I don't know until she gets to me and then I feel all right."

"If your mother were with you all night, you wouldn't have these bad dreams, would you?" I asked her.

"How did you know?" she asked, still whispering.

"Oh, I know," I replied. "Isn't it true?"

Rose nodded her head in a smiling assent.

"But your mother can't stay with you always, can she?" I asked. "You want her to have a little sleep, don't you, Rose?"

"Yes," answered the child, somewhat reluctantly.

"You see, Rose," I said, "one of the reasons why you have these bad dreams is because you want your mother to wake up in the night and look after you. But you don't have to prove that your mother loves you. She would be willing at any time to lose a whole night's sleep to look after you if you are really sick. But it wouldn't be fair, now would it, Rose, if you didn't let your mother get her rest at night when you really don't need her? Remember that you wake your daddy too."

Rose smiled at this and said, "But it is nice to feel mummy near me at night and daddy can sleep."

"But you see, Rose," I said, "you are growing up to be quite a young woman now. You will be going to school this year and when people grow up they don't make their mothers get up at night to look after them."

After a slight pause, I continued, "I have a little verse here, Rose, which I would like you to read to me."

I passed over to her a verse from the Bible that I had printed on a small card, knowing she could read printed words.

Slowly she read: "He shall feed his flock like a shepherd: he shall gather the lambs with his arm, and carry them in his bosom."[4]

"Tell me, Rose," I said, "who is the Good Shepherd?"

"Jesus is," she answered.

"And what does He do with the lambs?" I asked her.

"He carried them in His arms," Rose replied.

"Could any harm come to them when the Shepherd carried them in His arms?" I asked.

"Oh no. He keeps all bad things away," she answered.

"Now, Rose," I said, "when your mother hears your prayers and tucks you in at night, she is giving you her loving care and, because she must have some rest, she goes to bed a little later, but the Good Shepherd is watching over both you and your mother. You will not need to call your mother at night any more because now you know that the Good Shepherd will be looking after you. I want you to learn by heart the little verse I put on that card about the Shepherd gathering the lambs in His arms and carrying them in His bosom. Each night before you go to sleep, after you have said your usual prayers, I want you to say over and over again just as you are falling asleep, Good Shepherd, look after your little lamb tonight, and He will keep you in His arms."

The idea appealed tremendously to Rose and she gave ready assent to my suggestion. As she was going to sleep that night I stood at the door of the nursery and could hear her saying, "Good Shepherd, look after your little lamb tonight."

Every night at bedtime Rose said this prayer and the nightly terrors were completely vanquished. During several months she has not had a single nightmare and also by day she has been happier and more responsive to her mother.

The spiritual experience that can quiet and comfort the mind of a child will be a productive source of strength in later adult

[4] Isaiah XL:11.

years. Even those who through the greater part of their adult years are unaware of their childhood training in religion yet have something that will come back to them in the hour of crisis, just as one who has learned to swim in childhood and who has not practised the art for twenty or thirty years, on being thrown into the water by an accident or in shipwreck automatically makes use of his earlier experience and by using the strokes he learned in childhood manages to keep afloat until help reaches him.

I talked in a hospital one evening with a man who is an active and interested member of my church. He was recovering from a serious and painful illness, during which he had hovered between life and death. Relating some of his experiences, he said to me:

"I did not think that it was possible for a human being to endure as much suffering as I have experienced in the past three weeks. Do you know what it was that helped me keep a grip on myself when the pain was so intense that I was ready to let go of everything?"

"Please tell me," I said. "I should be most interested to know."

He said, "It was the Bible verses that I learned as a little boy at my mother's knee. One by one they all came back to me during those black hours when I needed them most of all. It was the realization of God's presence that I learned to know as a child which brought me through this dreadful experience."

"Train up a child in the way he should go: and when he is old, he will not depart from it." How often have those words been fulfilled in the experience of adults. The sense of fair play, truthfulness, honesty, integrity, honour, reverence, respect for the rights of others, which were inculcated in childhood have emerged in adult life and character.

Parental lack of interest in the religious development of their children is a key to both secular and religious problems. Mothers and fathers who would not think of neglecting the secular education of their children are in varying degrees indifferent to their religious training. They will often send their children to Sunday school without taking the trouble to inquire what they are learning there or whether or not their children know how to express in their daily lives the religious teaching which they receive.

Occasionally parents come to me and say: "It is impossible to interest my boy or my girl in Sunday school. They do not feel that they are getting anything out of it and I do not think that I ought to compel them to attend."

It is true, of course, that there are many Sunday schools in the nation with inadequately trained teachers and inefficient organization, but the basic trouble generally does not lie at this point. Boys and girls are very quick to sense the attitudes of the home, and, if the parents have little interest either in the religious experience of their children or in their own spiritual life, the children in turn soon become aware of this fact, and talk and act accordingly.

One does not find parents going to the principals in day-schools and saying: "I find it hard to interest my child in school. He does not want to go and I do not think I ought to compel him to attend."

As soon as parents in sufficient numbers insist upon their children having adequate spiritual training they will get it. Only as parents demanded secular education for their children did schools and universities develop.

The reason why parents oftentimes adopt an attitude to day-schools different from their attitude to Sunday schools is because they feel that an education in the day-school is absolutely essential to the future welfare of the child, but that a religious education is a matter of indifference.

No parent has the right to deprive his children of the stabilizing and strengthening influences which religion can exert in the life of even a very little child. In the years during which the foundations of character are being laid it is of tremendous importance that children should be brought into contact with the uplifting and inspiring influence of the personality of Jesus Christ. These are the years when their minds are easily richly stored with the moral precepts of the Bible and its lofty spiritual messages. Even though the meaning of these passages may not be wholly apparent to the children, they do include them in their young lives and the time will come when they are productive sources of spiritual strength, and help these young people, when they have grown into manhood and womanhood, to take their place in society as useful and worthy citizens and as men and women of God.

VIII. *The Confession and Forgiveness of Sin*

"Confess your faults one to another, and pray one for another, that ye may be healed. The effectual fervent prayer of a righteous man availeth much."

—James v:16

"If we say that we have no sin, we deceive ourselves, and the truth is not in us.

"If we confess our sins, he is faithful and just to forgive us our sins, and to cleanse us from all unrighteousness."

—I John 1:8, 9

"God be merciful to me a sinner."

—St. Luke xviii:13

"I, even I, am he that blotteth out thy transgressions . . . and will not remember thy sins."

—Isaiah xliii:25

"I acknowledged my sin unto thee, and mine iniquity have I not hid. I said, I will confess my transgressions unto the Lord; and thou forgavest the iniquity of my sin."

—Psalm xxxii:5

"As far as the east is from the west, so far hath he removed our transgressions from us."

—Psalm ciii:12

"Though your sins be as scarlet, they shall be as white as snow; though they be red like crimson, they shall be as wool."

—Isaiah 1:18

"Thy sins are forgiven. . . . Go in peace."

—Luke vii:48, 50

I RECEIVED a letter from a woman urgently requesting an interview. A large woman, with fair complexion and hair, about thirty-one years of age, she opened the conversation abruptly in the manner of one who had often told her story.

"I am a German," she said; "so is my husband. He is chief guard in a large bank which is owned and operated by Jews. I tell you this," she said, "because I think it may have something to do with my trouble, which is fear. My whole life is dominated by fear. It commenced," she said, "three years ago. For twelve months I have gone several times a week to a free psychiatric clinic. I have talked with the head doctor only three times, and in those instances for only five or ten minutes. Mostly assistant doctors looked after me. I have gone to a lot of other doctors in New York."

"How many doctors have you visited?" I asked her.

"Oh, I guess at least twenty in the last three years."

"I suppose I am safe in assuming that you did not obey their orders," I said to her. She made no reply.

I realized at once that the prospect of recovery is never hopeful in a case like this, where a person has been running from doctor to doctor. She would likely run from me.

Continuing her story she said:

"I am afraid when the door bell rings. I am afraid of the telephone. I am afraid that I am going to die from a heart attack. One of my friends died recently from a heart attack and the thing has never been out of my mind since. At night I lie awake and think that something is going wrong with my heart. It begins to palpitate and I have a sense of suffocation. At such times I am quite sure that sudden death is going to be my fate. Sometimes I have a notion that my husband has died during the night, and if he is lying perfectly still I reach over and touch him to make sure that he is still alive. I am afraid to stay in the house alone. I am afraid to go out of it alone. I am afraid to ride on buses or trams or trains."

"What do the doctors say is the trouble with you?" I asked.

"Well, in the main the doctors say that it is all a matter of nerves and that I shall have to learn how to master my nerves.

"I am afraid of my sister. If she doesn't come to visit me I am worrying as to what has happened to her. Is she sick? Has some accident happened? What has prevented her from coming? If she comes I am afraid of her and I tremble visibly with fear. I become so afraid that I will often put on a hat and coat and say that I have to go out for a minute. I call on a friend in the apartment and we go for a walk, for about ten minutes, and then I come back to talk with my sister. After my sister goes it takes me hours to recover from the nervous strain—I am so frightened of her."

"Why are you so afraid of your sister?" I asked her.

"I am afraid of her because she might tell the management of this Jewish bank that we are Germans. Jews have been boycotting the Germans and they might discharge my husband and then he will be unemployed."

"Well, why would your sister tell that?"

"I don't know why, but I am afraid of that. I don't see why she should, because I am helping to support her. Then I am afraid, also, that somebody else will tell the management of this bank that my husband is a German. That fear is constant.

"There is something else I want to tell you. A little more than three years ago a very dear brother of my husband's died suddenly. That affected my husband tremendously and he told me about it, but he didn't give me any details. He wanted to spare me because even then I was a little nervous, though not nearly so sick as I am now. My husband became a Christian after the death of his brother."

"Well, what effect did that have on your husband?"

"He became a different man."

"Did he tell you anything about his past?"

"Yes, he confessed that on two occasions he had been unfaithful to me. I went for a trip to Germany and I was away for six months and it was while I was away in Germany that my husband was unfaithful to me. The doctor had suggested this trip to Germany for my health, but I came back with the same nervous symptoms with which I left."

"Did you visit any doctors in Germany?"

"Yes, I visited at least three."

"And what did they say?"

"About the same things that the doctors in America told me."

Before she left at the conclusion of the first interview she said,

"There is one rather odd thing I want to tell you. When any of my friends come in and say, 'What time is it?' I look at the clock and say, 'It is twenty minutes past twelve.' Then, when the person has gone out, I look at the clock again and see that it was only seventeen minutes past. I become terribly uneasy until I can establish a contact with my friend, and then I say, 'I am very sorry I told you that it was twelve twenty o'clock. That was not true. It was twelve seventeen when you ·asked me the time.' "

In a later interview, at its commencement, she said,

"Do you remember a question you asked about my childhood? I told you that I was five years old then. Well, I am very sorry about this, but I was only four and a half."

"Well," I said, "what difference does it make whether you were four and a half or five?" And, referring to the statement she had made in a previous interview regarding her exactitude in reporting the time of day, I said:

"What difference did it make whether it was seventeen or twenty minutes past twelve?"

She said: "I suppose it didn't make any difference, but it troubled me a great deal."

"I am interested in this," I continued. "To me this is the most significant item in all the data you have given me. Why are you so anxious to convince people that you are telling the truth? Usually, when people are so meticulously honest in little things, it indicates that they are trying to divert attention from some major dishonesty or falsehood in their lives. Come now," I suggested, "be frank and tell me about the lie that you have been living."

She looked squarely at me and answered:

"There is nothing I know of."

I decided upon a different approach.

"What is there," I asked her, "that your sister knows about you which your husband does not? What is the thing that she knows or suspects and that you are afraid she will tell your husband?"

Again she replied:

"There is nothing that I know of."

I felt confident, however, that we had reached the crux of her problem and so I said to her:

"I notice that your brother-in-law's sudden death happened approximately at the time that your fear commenced."

This appeared to disturb her greatly and she said that she felt faint, which indicated to me that, as the children say in games, I was getting "warm."

"Did you know him very well?" I asked her.

She became more disturbed as she replied,

"Yes, fairly well."

"Now tell me," I said, "when your husband made his confession to you, didn't you feel very much like telling him about your wrong-doings? Before you have gone to sleep at night, haven't you often wanted to confess? Haven't you often envied the peace of mind and heart that he has had in his Christian experience? Wouldn't you give everything that you have in the world right now for the peace that comes from God's forgiveness and that takes fear out of our lives?"

"I most certainly would," she answered, beginning to cry.

"How many years ago was it, six or seven, when the improper relationship between you and your brother-in-law commenced?"

"Between six and seven," she said.

And then the full confession was poured forth from a surcharged heart. Her brother-in-law's death was a terrible shock to her and this was intensified by her husband's conversion and his frank confession to her of his own past sins. She had often wished to confess to him, but was afraid to tell him the truth. There was nobody to whom she would unburden her heart and all the time this suppressed sense of guilt and this inner tension were compelling her, while she lived a constant lie, to seek to assure everybody that she was scrupulously truthful and honest.

Prior to the onset of her nervous illness three years before, and because of her improper relations with her brother-in-law, there had existed in her an appropriate fear of discovery. This fear was natural and normal. It is altogether probable that unconsciously (or consciously) she had wished for her husband's death. Feeling guilty at these death wishes she suppressed them and they became transformed into the abnormal fear that her husband might die at any time. This would explain her reaching out during the night to assure herself that he was still alive. The repression of normal fears led to abnormal anxieties and inner tensions which eventually produced serious nervous disorders.

I requested her to kneel with me in prayer, and suggested that she ask God to blot out all the sins of her past. She replied:

"But I can't do that. I cannot make an audible prayer."

"Surely you can at least say, 'God be merciful to me, a sinner,'" I suggested.

"No," she said, "I can't say anything, not a word."

It was quite evident that her resistance at this point was due to the fact that for so long she had resisted the urge to confess the things that she had told me.

"I seriously doubt whether you can have a complete realization of God's forgiveness and his peace until you make that audible prayer," I said to her. "God's forgiveness and peace is given instantly to the truly penitent heart. Asking for forgiveness is the equivalent of receiving it."

Suddenly all her resistance gave way and she poured forth a prayer of penitance and confession, broken with sobs. She asked God to forgive her for the betrayal of her marriage vows, for the falsehoods told to her husband and her unfaithfulness to him, for the wrong that she had done to the wife of her brother-in-law and for breaking God's holy laws. Her contrition was overwhelming. When she had finished this prayer I suggested that she should now thank God for the unspeakable gift of His forgiveness and for the peace that was flooding her life. Audibly I added my thanksgiving to hers.

When we had risen from our knees her sobbing had stopped. She sat in her chair in complete relaxation. All the tension had gone. The healing power of God's forgiveness had brought to her serenity and peace. I quoted to her the message of God to St. Paul, "My grace is sufficient for thee: for my strength is made perfect in weakness,"[1] and explained to her that the grace of God had been bestowed upon her through the Divine forgiveness.

I explained to her the relationship between her sense of guilt and her fears and assured her that, little by little, she would gain the victory over the anxieties that had distressed her so long until some day she would be able to say with St. Paul, "When I am weak, then am I strong,"[2] that the time would come when the weakest point in her character would, by the help of God, become the strongest.

This woman, within four or five months of her first visit to my church, was not only able to travel by subway and bus alone in any part of the metropolitan area, something she had been unable to do for more than three years, but also she had fully resolved all her family conflicts.

I have talked with her on several occasions and find that she has made definite, steady convalescence from all her fears, abnormal anxieties, inner disquietude, heart trouble, and other symptoms produced by a repressed sense of guilt. She is now enjoying a normal, happy existence. I quote a paragraph from a letter she wrote to me several weeks after her confession:

[1] II Corinthians XII:9.
[2] II Corinthians XII:10.

"I am a great deal happier than I have ever been because Christ is now *very real* to me. At last I know the meaning of a mind at rest and a heart at peace. I keep constantly before me those verses you gave to me and they have helped greatly. Again I want to thank you for bringing Christ into my heart."

There is nothing so transforming for an individual as a first-hand experience of Christ. What is known in religious parlance as "conversion" is but the beginning of a process of spiritual development that moves steadily forward to its culmination in a Christian character victorious over all the ills of life.

When He enters a human life the dark and unwholesome tenants that have dwelt there are expelled. Here is an important point which is frequently misunderstood by psychiatrists who, unlike that distinguished member of the profession, Dr. Jung, are antagonistic to religion. Even psychiatrists who are tolerant of religion, whether or not they have strong faith themselves, know little or nothing about the healing power of faith. They are all sceptical about the fact of steady improvement in patients who get spiritual help from a minister, especially if inward renewal, with its accompanying physiological convalescence, comes about after only a few interviews with a minister.

A sense of guilt, deeply repressed, may produce all manner of symptoms of both nervous and physical disorders. A university student, twenty-three years of age, came to me complaining of great physical distress. When he went out-of-doors his vision became blurred. He suffered from loud drumming noises in his ears and a marked sense of dizziness overtook him as he walked along the street. His doctors found no physical basis for these symptoms.

A woman came in who had suffered for eighteen months from constant attacks of indigestion, indigestion not accounted for by any of several examinations by physicians.

Another woman had been under treatment by a physician for

neuritis of the left shoulder without improvement following. For eleven months she had been using hot applications without benefit.

A first-year medical student was driven almost frantic by symptoms of a mental disorder.

In this group of four cases just mentioned the mental and physical symptoms which had been produced in these persons by a repressed sense of guilt were immediately diminished after they had undergone an experience of the confession of sin and the acceptance of God's forgiveness similar to that of the woman who had been tortured by fears, the circumstances of whose case I have just described. All these physical symptoms were but a reflection of the maladies of the soul and completely disappeared within a period of from one to eight weeks.

Oftentimes the individual who is suffering from such symptoms as these does not connect them with the repressed sense of guilt. Sometimes it requires many interviews to make the individual aware of this relationship.

I know few errors more damaging to mental and physical well-being than a prolonged refusal to seek the relief and healing that is found in confession and forgiveness. Two years ago a woman came to me and in her first interview poured forth a confession. She had been married in New York for twenty years. Her husband occupied an important position in the business life of the city. They had no children. During all those years she had concealed from her husband the fact that a son had been born two years before her marriage to him. She had corresponded regularly with this son, who lived in a Southern state. All the letters were sent back and forth by a third party, so that the boy did not know his mother's name or her place of residence. She showed me his picture. He is a fine-looking young man and has been attending a university in the South. He goes by the name given to him by his mother many years ago.

For more than twenty years this woman has lived in constant fear that her guilty secret would be discovered, that somehow her son might learn her identity and come to New York to visit her, that her husband might come upon one of these letters from her boy, that somebody might make her true story known. The last thought in her mind before she fell asleep at night was the fear of detection, and the gnawing ache began the first thing each morning.

After twenty years of this mental torture she came to me for an interview. My past experience as a nurse in a mental hospital made it clear to me after my first meeting with her that confession had come too late, that already she was betraying definite psychopathic symptoms: she told me that often when she sat in a moving-picture theatre with her husband she saw that Hollywood had known her story and had woven it into the films, and in great distress she would get up and leave the theatre, making some excuse to her husband. She could not listen to the radio because, she said, the popular songs of the day were centred around her life's tragedy. She believed that people who rode on various occasions on the bus were talking about her, although they were total strangers.

I talked with this woman about God's willingness not only to forgive her sins of the past but to blot out the memory of them. Unfortunately, however, her mental deterioration had been so rapid that she seemed incapable of receiving the help that was offered to her. Constantly she would revert to the persecution she was receiving at the hands of Hollywood and repeatedly enquired whether or not I had any relationship to the moving-picture industry or had given any of the facts of her life to the producers. She is now an institution case. I am quite convinced that she would have evidenced an immediate improvement had she made her confession before the repressed sense of guilt had done irreparable damage to her mind.

Dr. C. G. Jung[3] stresses the helpful results that come from confession. He says:

"There appears to be a conscience in mankind which severely punishes the man who does not somehow and at some time, at whatever cost to his pride, cease to defend

[3] *Modern Man in Search of a Soul*, p. 39.

and assert himself, and instead confess himself fallible
and human. Until he can do this an impenetrable wall shuts
him out from the living experience of feeling himself a
man among men. . . . For we are all in some way or other
kept asunder by our secrets and instead of seeking through
confession to bridge the abyss that separates us one from
another we choose the easy by-way of deceptive opinion
and illusion."

Just as the continued repression of a sense of guilt produces
many and grave disorders, so does deliverance from it give to
the individual that serenity of spirit and that quietness and confidence which are so essential to mental and spiritual health.

It is important to remember, when dealing with the forgiveness of sins, that a man must not only seek God's forgiveness,
but also *he must be willing to forgive himself.* His opinion of
himself is far more important to him than the opinion of any
one else regarding him. Thoreau says, "Public opinion is a
weak tyrant compared with our private opinion." What we think
of ourselves is vital for our well-being. Self-contempt and self-
loathing are the source of many inferiorities and fears that
dominate the lives of men and women.

Everyone who has wronged himself or another punishes himself for his wrong-doing. In all of the cases that I have mentioned in this chapter the physical and mental distress which
each of these individuals suffered was in a large measure conscious, or unconscious, self-punishment. It was necessary for
me not only to lead these persons into the forgiveness of God,
but they had also to be persuaded to forgive themselves.

Sins which are forgiven ought also to be forgotten.

Time and again I have met men and women whose spiritual
progress was hindered by their constant turning back to sins of
the past. It is a great mistake to renew repentance for sins that
have been forsaken. One is frequently tempted to brood over
the past, to talk about its failures to others, to become accustomed to the backward look. All these practices are damaging
to the spiritual life.

Henry Ward Beecher has some very emphatic things to say on the subject of forgetting the sins that have been forgiven:

> "There are persons who live largely in rehashing their sins and their sense of guilt. Why, did you not repent of them? When a man has repented of his sins, that is enough. Put them out, do not keep them like so many mummies in the house. When you have done wrong and found it out, and have changed to right, and have rectified all the ways in which your wrong-doing has affected anybody else, that is the end: you have no business to come back and sit down on your old gravestones."

On another occasion, when he was referring to the practice of turning back to sins that had been repented of and forsaken, he says that such a practice

> "looked at from the standpoint of mere philosophy is not only false, but is mischievous to the last degree, and is not practical. We do not allow men to do that with their bodies. I have had men come to me from the war and want to regale me by showing where they were wounded; to take off the bandage and let me look at the sores. I was disgusted with them. There are a great many people who feel that the evidence of their piety needs to be shown by reciting their moral sores."

Robert Louis Stevenson, too, has some wholesome advice to give on this point:

> "Never allow your mind to dwell on your own misconduct. This is ruin. The conscience has morbid sensibilities. It must be employed but not indulged. One of the leading virtues is to let oneself alone."

If a modern *Pilgrim's Progress* were written and patterned on the lives of some present-day Christians, it would have to record that Pilgrim returned each day to take another look at the Slough of Despond. Rather ought we to follow the example of Bunyan's Pilgrim, who kept his eyes steadfast towards the

Celestial City. We should turn our faces resolutely away from our own weaknesses to the power of God that our minds may be filled with thoughts of holiness and victory. If we are willing not only to ask God for His spiritual gifts, but to take the gifts that He so freely gives, we shall obtain the needed strength and guidance.

Jesus warned us against the backward look when he said: "No man, having put his hand to the plough, *and looking back,* is fit for the kingdom of God."[4]

St. Paul echoed the Master's words when he said:

"This one thing I do, *forgetting those things which are behind,* and reaching forth unto those things which are before, I press toward the mark for the prize of the high calling of God in Christ Jesus."[5]

The Scriptures promise us that God not only forgives our sins, but that he remembers them no more against us for ever.

"I, even I, am he that *blotteth out* thy transgressions for mine own sake, and *will not remember* thy sins."[6]

"For I will forgive their iniquity, and *I will remember their sin no more.*"[7]

"Thou hast cast all my sins *behind thy back.*"[8]

Three elements are involved in an experience of the confession and forgiveness of sins. The first is contrition. When we have become contrite we acknowledge with sorrow the sins committed against God and the wrongs we have done to ourselves and our fellow-men. We acknowledge also the justice of God's judgment upon sin. One of the characteristics of impenitence is the refusal to acknowledge our guilt. We lay the blame on another as does Adam in the Genesis story when he says, "The woman whom thou gavest to be with me, she gave me of the tree, and I did eat."[9] We excuse our sins by saying that sin is inevitable and inescapable—an experience through which the

[4] St. Luke IX :62.
[5] Philippians III :13, 14.
[6] Isaiah XLIII :25.
[7] Jeremiah XXX :34.
[8] Isaiah XXXVIII :17.
[9] Genesis III :12.

human race must pass in its upward progress to a higher development. We may claim that it is due to the influence of our animal ancestry or, as a last resort, we may lay the blame on God and say with Omar Khayyám:[10]

> "Oh Thou, who Man of baser Earth didst make,
> And ev'n with Paradise devise the Snake:
>   For all the Sin wherewith the Face of Man
> Is blacken'd—Man's forgiveness give—and take!"

When we become truly contrite, however, we acknowledge that the responsibility for our sins is ours and ours alone. We say with the publican in Jesus' parable, "God be merciful to me a sinner."[11] We turn with shame and sorrow from sin to God.

In the second place, if we are truly contrite, we shall be ready to accept God's offer of forgiveness and to go forth after our confession, believing that we have received it. Full contrition on our part releases the forgiveness of God in us. We do not have to wait for it. It is instantaneous. When God forgives our sins His feelings and actions towards us are no longer determined by our past sin. This does not mean that all the penalties which sin brings upon the individual will immediately be annulled. There may remain both physical and mental consequences of sin, but our attitude to these is altered. They are no longer punitive, but have become wholly reformatory in their effects. Forgiveness also opens the way for the grace and power of God to flow into our lives, checking moral deterioration and creating a new quality of life and character.

In the third place, reparation or amendment for wrong-doing is a vital part of the experience of confession and forgiveness. The individual who is truly penitent will be ready, with God's help, to make all the restitution that is possible. So far as lies within his power he will seek to make good the wrong that he has done to other persons and to God. This will oftentimes involve writing letters of apology to persons whom his wrong-

---

[10] Fitzgerald's Translation.
[11] St. Luke XVIII:13.

doing has estranged and offended. It may mean that he will have to restore moneys unlawfully gained or relinquish honours to which he was not entitled.

He may find, in some instances, that it does not lie within his power to make restitution.

When Arthur Donnithorne, in George Eliot's story *Adam Bede*, goes back to Adam the carpenter and begs his forgiveness for having brought shame and ruin to Hetty Sorrell whom Adam dearly loved, the carpenter said, "There's a sort o' damage, sir, that can't be made up for."

But even in a case as extreme as that pictured by the novelist there is always something that can be done by way of reparation or amendment. Even if the victim of our transgressions should be beyond our reach, we can make amends to society itself and to God by consecrating all our energies to the promotion of righteousness and to ensuring that with the help of God whatever remains of life for us will not be lived in vain.

Why is there in man an urge to confess? Unquestionably it is due to the conscience—that inner monitor which speaks on behalf of the higher self and of God, and rebukes us for our wrong-doing. An awakened conscience can inflict torment upon the individual who refuses to confess. A striking illustration of this appeared in the *New York Times* of May 23, 1935. The incident occurred in Farmington, Missouri. The news item read as follows:

"Henry Huff, a fifty-year-old farmer, confessed today that he had killed a youth, who was his neighbour, thirty-one years ago.

"On May 24, 1904, the youth, Henry Mayes by name, was riding horseback on the highway when Huff intercepted him. There had been an argument, when Huff shot and killed the youth.

"When Huff went to the authorities with his confession, they said they did not know of any such crime. Only when the files were examined did they find this crime listed as one of the unsolved crimes of the state."

The most significant piece of information in the news item, however, is this:

> "Huff said that he had been tortured by his conscience and could not sleep, and was driven to confess. He waived all preliminary hearings and wished that sentence be pronounced as quickly as possible."

In the issue of the *New York Times* a year later another confession by a murderer is recorded. This time Charles Kohr, sixty-four years old, of Chicago, went to the authorities and declared that he had murdered his brother thirty-five years ago and was confessing it now because of the pangs of conscience. The most vital part of his confession was the words with which he concluded it:

> "I was even present at the inquest. I heard them decide the death was an accident. I carried that secret locked in my heart for thirty-five years—but I couldn't forget. I always knew that sometime I would have to tell."

How true are Matthew Arnold's words in *Tristran and Iseult*:

> There's a secret in his breast,
> Which will never let him rest.

The road to peace for all these tortured souls lies through the gateway of confession and forgiveness.

The confession of sin is not just an announcement to somebody of wrong-doing. That might be advertising or boasting. Some people endeavour to escape the costly experience of confession by talking about their sins to somebody who is equally guilty and who will offer no rebuke whatsoever. He who reveals his sin to any one but a minister of God is not "confessing" in the religious meaning of that word. He is telling it either in a social way, as in the instance of a friend, or in a professional way, as to a physician or a lawyer. Even he who talks about his sin to a minister may not *ipso facto* be telling it to God and even in telling it to God he may not be *confessing* it to God.

Physicians and lawyers play their parts in assisting individuals who are in trouble, but ordinarily they do not minister to the spiritual needs of the individual or point out the moral significance of so-called secular behaviour. Hence he who shows his wounds to others than a spiritual healer receives secular inspection and secular therapy.

Some people balk at a confession in the presence of a minister. This is especially true of Protestants. They have come to regard confession as a "Romish" practice and one to be abhorred. They cannot think of the experience of confession apart from the sacerdotal claims of the Roman Catholic Church. In the Protestant faith, however, the minister claims no power to forgive sins. He is present simply as God's agent and he brings to the penitent the assurances of God's forgiveness as these are set forth in the Scriptures.

A Protestant does well to remember that witnesses are present during the most important experiences of life. At his baptism there were witnesses. Witnesses must be present when he is married. And when he makes his last will and testament, which reminds him of the awful uncertainty and brevity of life, he must have witnesses as he records his name to the document. Why then should he hesitate about having a witness to the most solemn of all transactions between the soul and God?

I believe, also, that the Protestant conception of confession and forgiveness is more Scriptural because it is neither habitual nor compulsory, but voluntary. The individual comes to the minister not because the law of the Church says that he must, but because of an inner urge for confession and forgiveness.

No passage in the Scriptures can be adduced to substantiate compulsory confession. The one most frequently quoted for this purpose is James v:16: "Confess your faults one to another, and pray one for another, that ye may be healed. The effectual fervent prayer of a righteous man availeth much." But as Cardinal Cajetan fearlessly remarks, this passage enjoins only the mutual confession of Christians and the admission of special faults and not confession to a priest.

Apart altogether from other considerations, one of the advantages which the interviews of a Protestant minister with his people has over the Roman confessional is that the experience is a more costly one for the Protestant than it is for the Roman Catholic. In the Roman confessional the penitent is hidden from the priest each in a separate compartment with only a small opening between, which is screened, whereas the Protestant sits face to face with his minister.

Some penitents find that the direct gaze of a minister is further enquiry and they, therefore, bring out a fuller confession than would be the case were they not under direct scrutiny. Some priests ask few or no questions of the penitent and listen only to what is volunteered. Thus the parishioner who is able conveniently to forget some sins at a given moment may succeed in leaving without having confessed them.

The Protestant, sitting face to face with his minister and unveiling his heart in the presence of a fellow-human being as well as under the eyes of God, is undergoing an experience which, because it humbles his pride to the dust, is therefore more searching and cleansing in its effects.

The fact that confession for a Roman Catholic may be a less exacting experience than for a Protestant may explain the reason why some Catholics confess over and over again certain sins from which they have not found deliverance.

If the Catholic feels that confession to his own priest will be too great an ordeal he may go to a strange priest in another parish.

St. John of the Cross[12] has some pertinent observations at this point:

> "Many of them seek to be the favourites of their confessors, and the result is endless envy and disquietude. They are ashamed to confess their sins plainly, lest their confessors should think less of them, so they go about palliating them, that they may not seem so bad; which is excusing rather than accusing themselves. Sometimes they

[12] *The Dark Night of the Soul* I :II :4.

go to a stranger to confess their sin, that their usual confessor may think they are not sinners, but good people. And so they always take pleasure in telling him of their goodness, and that in terms suggestive of more than is in them : at the least, they wish all their goodness to be appreciated, when it would be greater humility on their part, as I shall presently show, to undervalue it, and wish that neither their confessor nor any one else should think it of the least importance."

There is another most important point of contrast between the Protestant and Roman Catholic use of the confessional. Unquestionably there are many faithful Catholics who make a legitimate use of the confessional and who find in it a fruitful source of spiritual consolation. The Roman Catholic priest gives much sound advice on moral problems to his parishioners. It is also true, however, that there are not a few cases in which an anxiety neurosis is developed in the minds of penitents who fear that they have not made a "good" confession and that they may incur the terrible penalty visited upon those who are guilty of this sin. This fear develops a dependent type of parishioner, who is constantly running back to the priest with unimportant data. It must be remembered, however, when the anxiety neurosis results in the penitent going, as some do, several times a day to a priest, that this would indicate that this so pronounced neurosis was not caused by visits to the priest but is one of many symptoms of a neurosis previously existing in the individual.

But the most vital point of difference in the uses of the confessional by Protestants and Catholics lies in the fact that the priest must listen to so many confessions, particularly on a Saturday, that many of them become simply part of a routine. Frequently the penitent confesses and the priest gives absolution for sins that are merely outward manifestations of and not the real cause of the spiritual malady in the life of the parishioner. The manner in which the confession is conducted and the limitations of time oftentimes render it impossible for the priest to enquire into the real causes of the individual's moral and spiritual downfall.

One of the most significant illustrations of this with which I have met was that of a Roman Catholic who is twenty-eight years of age and a teacher in a parochial school situated in a city other than New York. He had gone to his own priest to confess one week earlier, was in good standing with his church, and wanted to maintain his Roman Catholicism. He had listened to most of my addresses on the radio and came to see me, believing that I could help him.

The sin that troubled him was in the realm of sexual morals. He was deeply distressed and said:

"I have confessed this sin again and again. For a time I get along splendidly, but after a little while I go back to it once again. Then the situation becomes worse than before because I realize that I have broken the vows that I have made in the confessional and the promises of amendment."

He was so disturbed by his repeated failures that he had gone from parish to parish and priest to priest. In every case he had been dealt with kindly and, on making an act of contrition, had been given absolution.

After several interviews with this young man I discovered that there was a deeply rooted inferiority in his life that went back to his early childhood. Since I have dealt with inferiority in a separate chapter, no useful purpose would be served by enlarging upon the same subject here. He was the youngest of eleven children in the home and had never known any genuine achievement. All through life he had met with frustration and disappointment. The only realm in which he had experienced any measure of success was that of sex. This was his one source of satisfaction. He referred several times to the necessity of a youth possessing "manhood," as he termed his sex exploits.

After I had talked over the situation with him in several interviews he quickly grasped the fact that his sex affairs were in a large measure desperate attempts to escape from the feeling of inadequacy and to acquire what he considered evidence of his power over others—i.e., his supremacy. I pointed out to him that he had allowed his thoughts to turn far too often to this particular temptation and that by making repeated vows, which were always shortly broken, he had concentrated his mind steadily upon his own weaknesses instead of dwelling upon the power of God, by which victory would be achieved.

As we knelt in prayer in the consulting-room he reverently made the sign of the cross and expressed an act of contrition for the sins of the past, beginning as follows:

"O my God, I am heartily sorry for having offended Thee and I detest my sins most sincerely. . . ."

He concluded with a petition so moving that I wrote it down from memory after he had gone. It ran:

"O God, fill me with power that I may be strong to overcome my sins. Make me to know Thy purpose for my life. Help me to rise above every weakness and find in Thy service my happiness and my peace. Amen."

I gave to this young man one verse of Scripture—"I can do all things through Christ, which strengtheneth me"—and instructed him to fix his mind upon that text until he had made it a part of his life to seek to absorb its full significance, until the sense of God's presence and power in his life should fill his entire consciousness.

Day by day he continued to dwell upon the thought of Christ's power flooding his life and giving to him the victory over every temptation that assailed him. He soon discovered that he had progressed beyond the reach of the sins which formerly had brought about his moral downfall. At the same time, with increased confidence he went out of his way to meet people, to form new friendships, and to discover God's purposes for his life. His allegiance to his own Church has remained throughout unaltered and no slightest attempt has been made by me, at any time, to weaken it.

In my book *Fifth Avenue Sermons*[13] I have dealt with the

[13] Harper & Brothers, New York.

subject of the confession and forgiveness of sins in a sermon entitled "A Protestant View of the Confessional." Several points emphasized there are of sufficient importance to bear repetition:

"From the depths of the subconscious life there sometimes arise memories, emotions, impulses that express themselves in the conscious life of the individual, like bubbles that arise from the bed of a mill-pond and break upon the surface. They make their presence known in acute nervous disorders, decreasing efficiency in daily tasks, a sense of inferiority, phobias, and mental anguish that destroys the peace of mind and heart. The more he strives to repress these memories that cry out for a hearing the worse does the nervous condition of the patient become.

"In every case where the trouble is due to past transgressions the sovereign remedy is a full and complete confession. That alone can bring the realization of God's forgiveness, with inward cleansing and peace.

"Shakespeare, who plumbed the depths of human emotions, understood how desperate may be this need. In his tragedy *Macbeth* we see Lady Macbeth, after the murder of Duncan, King of Scotland, tortured by a guilty conscience. In her dreams, where the subconscious mind holds sway, she sees again the stain of the dead king's blood on her hands. She walks in her sleep, frantically trying to efface this evidence of her guilt.

" 'Out, damned spot! Out, I say! . . .
Here's the smell of blood still;
All the perfumes of Arabia will not sweeten
this little hand.'

"Macbeth, who has been watching his wife, says to the attendant physician:

" 'Canst thou not minister to a mind diseas'd,
Pluck from the memory a rooted sorrow,
Raze out the written troubles of the brain,

> And with some sweet oblivious antidote
> Cleanse the stuff'd bosom of that perilous stuff
> Which weighs upon the heart?'

"To which the physician replies:

" 'Therein the patient must minister to himself.'

"The great dramatist was right. Each of us holds in his hand the key to his own happiness. Only he can unlock the secret door that allows the peace of God to enter and find a dwelling-place in his heart. . . .

"Any minister who has looked deep into human hearts will not be deluded, by the placid exterior of men and women, into thinking that few people have problems to distress them. He has learned, from experience, that in a multitude of human lives there is restlessness, nervous tension, inner confusion, and disintegration of character. He knows, too, that to him has been entrusted a message that can bring into these disoriented lives healing, serenity, and peace."

In every individual there is usually one supreme weakness, one temptation that comes upon him with compelling force, one sin that seeks to capture the citadel of the soul. It may be drink or sex—most obvious sins of the flesh. Or it may be the more subtle sins of spiritual pride, uncharitableness, cherished resentments, or a forthgoing bitterness towards others which springs from a desperate inner need of healing and peace. But whatever the sin may be and howsoever it may manifest itself, the unfailing remedy is penitence, confession, restitution, and an experience of the forgiveness of God which lifts the burden of guilt from a heart that has been crushed by its desolating weight.

It is impossible for any one adequately to describe the exhilaration of spirits, the sense of liberation and release that comes to one who has undergone an experience of the confession and forgiveness of sin.

A construction engineer, who for twelve months had been

tortured by his conscience, confessed that he had been unfaithful to his wife. His penitence was overwhelming and the transformation wrought on him by his acceptance of God's forgiveness was correspondingly great. He said to me weeks later,

"God's forgiveness has changed my life. Barriers have gone down in my home and I have a far greater love for my wife and children than I have ever known before. Also, I am able again to pray."

A social worker, who had experienced the forgiveness of God, declared to me afterward that her attitude towards the people whom she served had undergone a complete change.

"Whereas at one time," she said, "I regarded them merely as a nuisance, now I find myself taking a personal interest in the welfare of every one of them as the children of God."

A man engaged in educational work confessed to a sin that had wrecked his peace for five years. Having received and accepted God's forgiveness, he said:

"God has entered my life again, freed me of my sin and made my relationship to my mother better than it has ever been before. I can look her in the eye now for the first time in five years and I meet her as I face the world, holding my head up again. God is my Friend and everyone's Friend who will have Him."

An experience of God's forgiveness reaches out and affects all relationships. First is its reaction upon the forgiven individual. Any one who has truly confessed his sins and sought the forgiveness of God will not long be in doubt as to the reality of the experience. He feels within him the stirrings of the new life. He has made a new beginning, a fresh start. He has burned the bridges behind him. He has crossed the Rubicon. The prison doors are open. His shackles have fallen off. Courage and faith are kindled in his heart. Disabling fear is vanquished. Doubts are swept away. His life is flooded with happiness and peace not as he had known before but abundant now, in the will and love of God.

Secondly, there is a changed relationship to God. No longer does the forgiven man feel that God is against him. He is reconciled to God. When a man forgives some one who has wronged him, it is as though he says to him, "I no longer hold against you what you have done to me. I have forgotten it. My feelings towards you are as though the wrong had not been done." So is it in his relationship with God. When his sins are forgiven God's attitude towards him is no longer determined by his sin. Many men and women continue to be defeated by sin because they know that it stands unconfessed and unforgiven between them and God. It shuts off the vision of God as a black cloud conceals the face of the sun. It makes fellowship with God impossible. But forgiveness changes all this. It restores communion with God, and the sins that stood between the sinner and Him are "blotted out," are "put behind His back," are "remembered no more for ever," are "removed as far as the east is from the west."

In the third place, the forgiven man's relations to his fellow-men are changed. Usually, the transformation is evidenced first of all in his home. Where antagonisms and tensions once reigned, love and peace now abide. The spirit of goodwill reaches out into all his business and social relationships. The love which has been kindled in his heart towards God is now finding expression in love to his fellow-men. To him the words of the Psalmist may fittingly be applied:

"Oh the bliss of him whose guilt is pardoned,
        and his sin forgiven!
    Oh the bliss of him whom the Eternal has absolved,
        whose spirit has made full confession!"[14]

[14] Psalm XXXII:1, 2. Moffatt's Translation.

IX. *Pastoral Psychiatry*

"Now when the sun was setting, all they that had any sick with divers diseases brought them unto him; and he laid his hands on every one of them, and healed them."

—St. Luke iv:40

"And all things, whatsoever ye shall ask in prayer, believing, ye shall receive."

—St. Matthew xxi:22

"For God hath not given us the spirit of fear; but of power, and of love, and of a sound mind."

—II Timothy 1:7

"Peace I leave with you, my peace I give unto you: not as the world giveth, give I unto you. Let not your heart be troubled, neither let it be afraid."

—St. John xiv:27

"Beloved, let us love one another: for love is of God; and every one that loveth is born of God, and knoweth God. He that loveth not knoweth not God; for God is love . . . and he that dwelleth in love dwelleth in God, and God in him."

—I John iv:7, 8, 16

PASTORAL PSYCHIATRY, as I have already defined it in the Introduction to this book, is the ministry of pastors directed to the healing of the soul. It is distinguished from the practice of the psychiatrist and the physician by the fact that the pastor works to bring his parishioner into contact with God and the spiritual resources that flow from Him. A minister devoted to the service of God has neither the intention nor the desire to limit himself to the work of either the psychiatrist or the physician.

Interestingly enough, all physicians throughout the world come nearer to being unofficial agents of God than they are aware. It is of no import that some of them have no consciousness of a mission for God or that others perhaps might, in a questionnaire, call themselves agnostic. The Prophet Isaiah informed the pagan ruler Cyrus that he was an agent of God even though Cyrus owed no allegiance to Israel's God. The word of Jehovah reported to Cyrus was this:

"I girded thee, though thou hast not known me."[1]

Not all those who work for God are aware that their service is being rendered to Him. Physicians and surgeons labour for years, sometimes for a lifetime, in hospitals endowed by churches or religious benefactors—hospitals that sometimes are even branches of religious institutions. Whether or not medical men are willing to admit it, they are nonetheless carrying on the traditional work of leaders in hygiene, medicine, and religion of both the Old and the New Testament. When a physician happens to be the eldest son of a Jewish rabbi, he is born a rabbi. Some have elected to enter the priesthood or the Protestant ministry and many are doing the work of God with-

[1] Isaiah XLV:5.

out being aware of the fact. Regardless of how physicians may consider it, the daily work of a general practitioner of medicine contains very much in it that ministers of religion think of as service not only rendered to man but also to God.

Most individuals and almost all professions working for the benefit and comfort of others have definite limitations as to the type of people whom they serve. This is not true, however, of physicians and surgeons. In peace and in war they place no restriction upon the race, religion, nationality, morality, or economic condition of their patients. A Jewish surgeon, for instance, would not hesitate to give to the very limit of his knowledge and his skill in the service of a Jew-baiting Nazi. The attitude of physicians and surgeons in this respect approaches close to the ideal set forth by the Master:

> "That ye may be the children of your Father which is in heaven: for he maketh his sun to rise on the evil and on the good, and sendeth rain on the just and on the unjust."[2]

In all these ways the work of physicians overlaps that of priests and of ministers. On the other hand, when a pastor brings spiritual resources to bear upon the sick, regulating and stabilizing physiological processes, then the work of the minister overlaps that of the physician.

No matter what happens to be manifest at any given moment in the relationships of ministers and physicians, there exists nevertheless latently a community of interests, techniques, and goals. When either the minister or the doctor seeks a better degree of coöperation between their respective professions, each may know that already there exists a basis for such coöperation.

The harmonious interrelationship of ministers and medical men can best be achieved when both realize that while each group has a distinct function to fulfil, their ministrations overlap and the effectiveness of each is enhanced by working in harmony with the other.

A well-instructed pastor does not attempt to diagnose any form of physical or mental disorder, or suggest treatment for

[2] St. Matthew v:45.

these illnesses. He declines to deal with people who show definite psychopathic symptoms and who come to him instead of to a doctor. He refers them at once to a physician or a psychiatrist. "Has a doctor prescribed for you?" and, "Are you carrying out his orders carefully?" are questions that ought often to be on the lips of the pastor. His ministrations to sick souls, and indirectly to sick minds and bodies, will be best carried on as he works in close coöperation with physicians. He will recognize in the discoveries and methods of modern medicine something of the purposes of God for human well-being as he sees these purposes manifested also in spiritual regeneration.

Physicians, on the other hand, will not be slow to recognize as an ally, in their fight against disease, a spiritual ministry that quiets the mind, reinforces the will, and brings confidence and peace into the hearts of their patients.

The physician works with the body, the psychiatrist with the mind, the pastor with the soul. But soul, mind, and body act and react upon each other. The body influences the mind, the mind reacts upon the body, and the health or unhealth of the soul will have a determining influence on both mind and body. Many disorders of body and mind are due to maladies of the soul with which only a spiritual ministry is equipped to deal.

In the preceding chapter on the confession and forgiveness of sins I have cited several illustrations of the profound disturbances caused in the minds and bodies of men and women through a deeply-rooted sense of guilt produced by sin—disturbances which were relieved only as these individuals became reconciled to God through confession and forgiveness and thus found themselves once more in right relationship with their fellow-men.

The minister who brings men and women into a vital contact with God, who teaches them how to use the Bible for spiritual development, how to meditate, how to pray, how to develop a strong and radiant faith, will be rendering an incalculable service to the minds and bodies of his parishioners as well as to their souls.

Dr. David W. Mackenzie, senior, a foremost Canadian surgeon, of Montreal, in his presidential address to the American Urological Association in June, 1938, reminded his hearers that the patient is a soul as well as a body:

"Sir Thomas Browne said three hundred years ago in *Religio Medici*, that he could not go to cure the body of his patient but he forgot his profession and called unto God for his soul. Today in our practise we need to remember that the patient is to be regarded as a soul as well as a body, that human beings are mental and spiritual as well as physical organisms. We need to remember this all the more because in our day the emphasis on early specialization and on over-specialization tends to make us forget it. Our medical books and our entire medical education are not blameless in this respect. We need in our treatment to restore some of the viewpoint of the old and vanishing family physician while not sacrificing important and necessary values, or the benefit of concentration in special fields. We must remember, above all, the totality of the patient.

". . . The doctor may forget that it is his duty and indeed his ideal, to assure the patient not only health of body when possible, but also peace of mind and soul. What matters most, after all, is the patient's comfort and happiness. Our treatment is not an end in itself, it is a means to an end: and that end is the patient's comfort and happiness and peace. Life is basically a keeping of body and soul together and the good of the two is inseparable. Human nature includes spirit and body and we have to deal with both in their interrelations; only by such an attitude and such methods can we attain our best results and realize our highest ideals."

In the past physicians, as a rule, have been somewhat diffident in acknowledging that the patient is a soul as well as a body or in admitting the value to the patient of a spiritual ministry. This is due in part to the fact that their training in the medical school has been largely materialistic. Many physicians would be embarrassed to admit how little they know about religion and how much or how little of it in their own experience is unlabeled and unidentified. They usually avoid inquiring into their patients' religious interests and activities, lest the patients spread abroad the doctor's interest in religion as being appropriate or inappropriate to the patient or to the doctor himself. But surely all this is determined by the way in which the doctor speaks. He is able to talk freely to his patient on other topics that he believes are beneficial to him. One wonders, therefore, why he does not discuss religion, when the occasion warrants it, without reluctance or hesitation.

Again, doctors are afraid lest, when they have committed themselves publicly with regard to the value of religious faith in the work of healing, some of the more recent religious cults that crowd the borderland between science and superstition should take advantage of their statements in an unfair manner to promote their own causes.

Some physicians, too, have had unfortunate experiences with ministers who have actually been tactless in the sick-room thereby exciting and distressing the patient by their visit. In such cases the physician quietly passes the word on to the family and the nurse that there are to be no more visits from this pastor, and then he transfers his disapproval of one on to the whole number of ministers and sometimes to religion itself.

Nevertheless, not a few physicians and surgeons believe in God, carry on the daily practices of religion, and observe and encourage in their patients constructive spiritual activity.

I talked with a physician who is chief anæsthetist in a large general hospital. Out of the experience of twenty-five years administering anæsthetics to many hundreds of people annually, he said:

"For a long time I have observed the mental and spiritual attitude of patients coming to the operating-room. This is, of course, a serious moment for them all. Many times I have noticed their lips moving in prayer just as I was about to adjust the mask to give them the anæsthetic."

"What would you say," I asked him, "about the effect of religious faith on persons who are about to undergo an operation?"

"I have noticed," he responded, "that persons with a strong religious faith have far less dread of the operation beforehand and a smaller measure of surgical shock after the operation. Many surgeons would testify to this."

"Is there any difference," I asked him, "in the way in which persons with a calm religious faith take the anæsthetic in comparison with those who face the ordeal on their own resources?"

"This is the point at which I have noticed the greatest difference," he answered. "Patients who go to the operating-table with a confident faith in God take less anæsthetic, recover from it more easily and with far less of the usual distressing after-effects. They have little or no restlessness or post-operative fever. They go through the crisis of acute disease more easily and have a quicker and less eventful convalescence. They carry out the doctor's orders better and coöperate more freely with the nurses and other members of the hospital staff."

Leaders of thought in the Christian Church of our day have for many years been drawing the attention of ministers to this fruitful field of service. For instance, Dr. W. R. Inge, until recently Dean of St. Paul's Cathedral, London, writing to the English Press, says:[3]

> "I hope that in the future the clergy will regard themselves primarily as physicians of the soul. The proper study of mankind is man; and there is no more fascinating study than the varieties of human nature. . . .
>
> "I should like to see the practice of private consultation much more developed, and treated more as a matter of course, than it is in the Protestant churches. A clergyman who has tact, experience, and real sympathy can do much more good in this way than by his public ministrations.
>
> "If we were set to fill a number of narrow-necked vessels with water—and we are all narrow-necked vessels—should we set them up in rows and dash a bucket of water over

[3] *Daily Telegraph,* London, September 25 and October 2, 1934.

them? That is the method of the pulpit. A few drops may get in here and there, but most of the water is wasted. . . . The most important part of a clergyman's work should be that of physician of the soul. The Church has neglected that important part of a clergyman's duty—consultation. It ought to be a matter of course for our people to come to us when they are in difficulties about their souls."

The value of this coöperation for which Dr. Inge pleads has been demonstrated to me again and again in my pastoral ministry.

On one occasion I was called to the home of a parishioner who had shortly to undergo a very critical thyroid operation. When I visited her she recalled an interview she had had with me six months earlier. On that occasion she had opened the conversation by saying:

"For eighteen years I have lived in New York, attending church fairly often, but in all that time until now no minister has ever asked me if I had a soul and no minister has shown the slightest personal or even impersonal interest in my spiritual welfare. Since you came to this church a year ago I have attended it more regularly, but I have not yet obtained happiness and peace from my religion. One trouble in most churches is that they do not offer personal help to their members. Ministers continually exhort us to do right, but the greatest difficulty for me, and I think I could say for all of us who sit in the pews, is to learn *how* to do that which we ought and really want to do; how to make the Christian faith fully effective in our own lives."

"Tell me specifically what you have in mind," I said to her.

"Well, take my own case," she said. "I have a husband and a fine daughter, but I am not the help to them I ought to be. I am concerned so much with my own troubles and worries that I have become more of a burden than an assistance to them all."

Then she proceeded to tell me of a conflict that had arisen with her husband's brothers over certain family matters. She had a strong feeling of resentment against them, which pro-

duced definite symptoms of nervous tension and strain in herself. In the interviews that followed she sought and found the
spiritual resources necessary to overcome this feeling of resentment and so became reconciled to her husband's relatives.
The passage of Scripture which helped her most in securing
her emancipation from resentment and ill will was from Colossians,[4] which in Moffatt's translation reads as follows:

> "As God's own chosen, then, as consecrated and be-
> loved, be clothed with compassion, kindliness, humility,
> gentleness, and good temper—forbear and forgive each
> other in any case of complaint; as Christ forgave you, so
> must you forgive. And above all you must be loving, for
> love is the link of the perfect life. Also, let the peace of
> Christ be supreme within your hearts—that is why you
> have been called as members of the one Body."

Daily she set apart a period for the reading of the Bible and
prayer. This spiritual discipline gave to her serenity and peace
which hitherto she had not known. The result was manifested
in a happier family life.

On the occasion of the visit to which I have reference now,
I came at the request of her husband.

He told me that the surgeon in charge of his wife had prepared him for the worst.

"I want you to know," he had said, "that your wife's condition is exceedingly critical. Our greatest difficulty will be with
her nervous condition which affects her heart. She was so
frightened at the time of the last operation that we had difficulty bringing her through. She must now have complete rest,
with absolutely no visitors until after the operation."

The husband fully valuing the surgeon's solicitude for his
patient, nonetheless earnestly desired me to visit his wife. She
herself wanted to talk with me. So I suggested that I should
first see the surgeon personally to get his permission to visit her.

When I talked with the doctor it was quite apparent that he
was not cordial towards ministers. He had had one or two
unfavorable experiences of their visitations in hospital wards.

[4] Colossians III:12-15.

"This woman has a very weak heart," he said to me. "At the time of her two previous operations she was so nervous and her pulse was so rapid that in each case I considered delaying the operation. I'm afraid that if you talk to her about spiritual things it will distress her and increase her nervous tension."

I suggested to the surgeon that, if he found after my second or third visit that there was no improvement in his patient's nervous condition, I would not call on her again until after the operation. He agreed to this arrangement with some reluctance.

On visiting her home I found her resting in bed.

"Well, here I am," she said, "troubling you again. I have been very happy in my new religious experience, but now it is being tested to the limit. In three weeks' time I have to go to the hospital for another thyroid operation. In the last five years I have had two such operations and I find myself dreading this one. I hate to think of the ride in the ambulance, of lying for weeks in a hospital bed, and experiencing again all the noises and the smells that go with a hospital. Whenever I picture to myself the nurse preparing me again for the operating-room, I break out in perspiration and my heart palpitates until it almost chokes me. I'm afraid that I haven't been a real Christian long enough to build up a faith that will stand the test of this ordeal."

As she was speaking I noted the deadly pallor of her face and lips and her hands that trembled as she talked of the operation that lay ahead.

"What do you fear most of all about the hospital and the operation?" I asked her. "Are you afraid to die?"

"No, it is not that," she answered, "but just the very thought of the hospital drives me into a panic."

I picked up her Bible which lay on a table by the bedside, and turning to the thirty-fourth Psalm read these words:

> " 'I sought the Lord, and he heard me, and delivered me from all my fears.'[5]

[5] Psalm XXXIV:4.

"Here is a man," I said to her, "whose life was filled with fears. He went to God for help and found the deliverance that he sought, until the day came when he could confidently assert these words I am reading to you now:

> " 'I sought the Lord, and he heard me, and delivered me from all my fears.'

A little later on in the chapter," I said to her, "the Psalmist gives us a clue as to what happened. He writes:

> " 'The angel of the Lord encampeth round about them that fear him, and delivereth them.' "[6]

"But doesn't it say," interjected the woman, "that he feared God?"

"Yes, it does," I replied, "but there is a vast difference between fearing God and being afraid of Him. When the fear of God is spoken of in the Bible, the word 'fear' means reverence towards God and submission to His will. He was not afraid of God, but he yielded himself completely to whatever God willed for him. 'The angel of the Lord'—that is, God's presence—was round about him and he became so sure of God that he lost his fears."

The eyes of the sick woman brightened with interest.

"Isn't that strange! I had never thought of that. Now I see where my trouble has been. I have been thinking so much about myself and what might happen to me that I have forgotten about God. From now on I am going to concentrate on the thought of God's presence until it becomes real to me and I am sure that I, too, will get deliverance from my fears."

I visited my parishioner the night prior to her operation, the surgeon having told the nurse to admit me whenever I should come. Before I left her she said to me:

"The most wonderful thing in the world has happened to me. My fears are gone. I can say just as truly as the Psalmist did:

> " 'I sought the Lord, and he heard me, and delivered me from all my fears.' "

* Psalm XXXIV:7.

The operation took place at nine o'clock the following morning. At five in the evening I visited her room and found her recovered from the anæsthetic and resting quietly. She was not permitted to speak, but her eyes smiled a welcome. I paused beside her bed for less than a minute, repeating to her the words that had become so familiar and so precious in her experience:

> " 'The angel of the Lord encampeth round about them that fear him, and delivereth them.' "

Momentarily she closed her eyes as I recited these words and when she opened them the light of a great peace shone forth.

Three days later I talked with her husband, who was delighted at the splendid progress which his wife was making.

"I met the doctor today," he said, "and he is tremendously pleased with my wife's convalescence. He said to me: 'Really, it was the most extraordinary thing I have ever seen. We had been so anxious about the nervous condition of your wife that we rather dreaded the morning of the operation. She had been very peaceful for the last week or two but I had felt that it couldn't last. Do you know that at the very moment when we were ready to administer the anæsthetic, her pulse was as steady as a clock. There is no doubt about her ultimate recovery.' "

Some weeks later, when I talked over with my parishioner her experiences at the hospital, she said to me:

"I have never gone to my bed at night after a happy day with a greater feeling of peace than was in my heart when I lay upon the operating-table. God's presence was more real to me even than that of the doctor and nurses. The last thought in my mind was the words of that text:

> " 'I sought the Lord, and he heard me, and delivered me from all my fears.' "

Everyone familiar with hospital routine knows that surgeons demand an unvarying ritual of preparation for an operation in the case of each patient. There are no exceptions. This preparation is of almost equal importance with the operation itself.

I believe that, in addition to the physical preparations unvaryingly made before each surgical operation, there is indicated also definite spiritual preparation. There are few moments in human experience when the need for a spiritual ministry is so urgent as in those trying and critical hours when one is awaiting an operation. Then, if ever, one needs to draw upon spiritual resources of quietness and confidence. Then, if ever, the relatives, too, who are fearfully awaiting the beginning and the end of an operation upon a dear one, need the upholding power of these selfsame spiritual resources. How steadying to them in such an hour of crisis is the promise of God set forth by His Prophet:[7]

"In quietness and in confidence shall be your strength."

Everyone who has undergone an operation is aware of the tremendous comfort that is given to him by the knowledge that those near and dear to him are upholding him and themselves with their prayers. A patient in a New York hospital said to me a week or two after her operation:

"Shortly before I went to the operating-room I had a telephone call from my brother three hundred miles away. In a few simple words he assured me of his love and of his constant prayers before, during, and after the operation."

Her eyes filled with tears as she said:

"No human being can ever understand how much that message meant to me. I remembered that even as my brother's love went out to me, so also was I surrounded and upheld by the love of God. It seemed to me that God's love filled and possessed my entire consciousness. I was not emotionally disturbed, but all fear was vanquished and I believe I experienced what the Bible means when it speaks of the peace that passeth understanding."

Spiritual peace is inclusive of and over and above secular calmness. One observes people, without any religious beliefs and sometimes definitely hostile to religion, approaching an operation with a large measure of calm. Any individual with

[7] Isaiah xxx:15.

great strength of will can, by exerting it to the utmost, steel himself to meet the inevitable. There is also the calm that comes from despair. Human beings can bring themselves to face almost any fate when once they realize that there is no possibility of escaping it.

Spiritual quietness and calm, on the other hand, well up from within. The heart possessed by love for God and love for its fellows has nothing to fear. Nothing can come to God's child save what the Father wills, and His will is accepted without rebellion and without fear.

> "Thou wilt keep him in perfect peace, whose mind is stayed on thee, because he trusteth in thee."[8]

This peace differs from secular calm in that it is a peace that the world cannot give us and cannot take from us. Secular calm is so often at the mercy of one's environment. A slight change in circumstances—financial loss, the death of a friend, or some other happening may wreck it instantly, but the heart and mind that is stayed on God possesses deep within it a peace untroubled, unshaken, untouched by all the storms that rage.

What new advances might not be possible in hospitals and especially in operating-rooms if all patients went through the ordeal of illness with their minds stayed upon God and with His peace in their hearts; and if all doctors and nurses were upheld by a faith akin to that which is set forth in the *Religio Medici* of Sir Thomas Browne!

Some modern healing cults make large use of suggestion. It will do little good, however, to suggest to an individual that all is well with him if, in his own mind and heart, he is guilty before God. Suggestion is not a magic wand with which we can cause the misdoings of the past to disappear, or obliterate them from the memory. In the preceding chapter we have seen how only the healing power of God's forgiveness can provide a therapy for hearts and minds that have borne for long the burden of guilt. The Bible goes beyond suggestion:

[8] Isaiah XXVI:3.

"The Lord is my shepherd; I shall not want."[9]

"Who forgiveth all thine iniquities; who healeth all thy diseases."[10]

"If God be for us, who can be against us?"[11]

"Thanks be to God, who giveth us the victory."[12]

"I can do all things through Christ who strengtheneth me."[13]

When these great religious affirmations are uttered thoughtfully and feelingly as an assertion of faith, they have a profoundly stimulating influence upon the life of him who makes them his own. But this is not mere suggestion. It is not merely the expression of a hope. It is the confident assertion of faith that lays hold of the blessing that is desired and appropriates it. "He restoreth my soul," says the Psalmist. The restored soul in turn stimulates, renews, reinvigorates the mind and the body.

Spiritual stimulation not merely facilitates physiological and mental activities, but it also regulates them. In the instance of the woman who had to undergo a thyroid operation, spiritual stimulation steadied and regulated her heart beat. In earlier chapters there is abundant illustration of the manner in which spiritual stimulation composes and quiets the mind. It is from God who alone can heal and restore the soul.

Generally, pastors will be well advised not to extend their ministry to the mentally sick unless they have been requested to do so by a physician or psychiatrist. And even then they should do so only after having sought the doctor's advice on how best to approach the patient. A larger measure of freedom in this matter can safely be exercised only by such pastors as have had a thorough and practical training in dealing with mental cases.

Even in the instance of people who are definitely classed as insane, if previous to their illness they have had a strong re-

[9] Psalm XXIII:1.
[10] Psalm CIII:3.
[11] Romans VIII:31.
[12] Corinthians XV:57.
[13] Philippians IV:13.

ligious faith, a spiritual ministry can frequently bring them comfort and peace.

On one occasion I visited the home of a parishioner whose mother had just come from a mental hospital. She was pronounced harmless and the superintendent of the hospital told the family that if a nurse were put in charge of her she could be kept quite well at home. I suggested to her son, a physician, that I should like to talk with his mother. He said:

"There isn't a bit of use. You won't be able to reach her at all. She seems to have lost contact with her surroundings and has forgotten about her earlier years."

"In any case," I said to him, "I should like to see your mother because you have just told me about her strong religious faith and I have oftentimes discovered that, when all other approaches to the individual are closed, one may gain access through the patient's religious experience."

"Very well," he said. "It certainly won't do mother harm, at any rate."

He led the way into her room, where his mother and her nurse were seated. She paid little or no attention to us and scarcely seemed to notice our presence. I said to her:

"Do you know this man?" pointing to her son.

She looked up for a moment with a weary expression on her face and said:

"I don't know him."

"Isn't this your son George?" I said.

"No," she answered. "He looks a little like my boy, but it isn't he. I wish somebody would take me to my home and my people. Everything is strange here. Nothing is the same any more."

All the while, as she talked, she kept wringing her hands and moaning piteously.

"Take me where I'll know somebody," she said. "Everything is strange here."

At that very moment she was in what had been her sitting-room for twenty years before the onset of her illness.

"Tell me," I said to the mother, "how many brothers and sisters did you have?"

She passed her hand across her forehead with a nervous and tired gesture and said:

"I don't know. I can't remember."

"You had two brothers and two sisters, hadn't you?" I suggested, recalling information given to me by her son.

"I don't know," she replied. "Perhaps I had. I can't remember."

"Can you tell me," I asked her, "which was the older of the two, George or Harold? Come now. You often played with them when you were children. Do you remember which was the older?"

"I don't know," she said, wearily. "I can't remember. I can't remember anything. I am all confused and everything is new and strange here. Take me home to my own people."

I asked her a few additional questions about her earlier home life, but failed to elicit any response. At this point her son said:

"I have often tried to get mother to recall something of her earlier years, but without result. We cannot seem to touch the springs of memory. She has forgotten everything."

At this point I turned to his mother and said:

"Your son has told me of the strong religious faith you have had, of your love for the church and its services, and of the interest you have had in your Bible and in prayer. I would like to remind you that, even if you feel that your surroundings have changed, one thing remains the same. God has not changed. He never changes. People may change and surroundings may change, but God abides the same forever."

For the first time I saw that she was really listening to me. I talked to her about God's unchanging love and that wherever we may be we can always find Him and enter into fellowship with Him.

At my request the doctor brought me his mother's Bible. I sat down beside her with the Bible open before us and turned over the pages of it, directing her attention to passages in it that she herself had marked. One especially had been deeply underscored. It was the last verse of the thirty-fourth Psalm. I read it to her:

> " 'The Lord redeemeth the soul of his servants: and none of them that trust in him shall be desolate.' "

"That verse must have meant much to you," I said, speaking slowly with short sentences. "You marked this yourself. It is your Bible. God will not leave you desolate. God is very near to you. I am going to leave your Bible open at this passage. Please read that verse again after I have gone."

She was listening attentively now. Then I continued:

"I am going to repeat to you a very familiar Psalm.[14] You have known and loved it for a long time. Listen to me:

" 'The Lord is my shepherd;' " Instantly she broke in, saying, " 'I shall not want.' "

" 'He maketh me to lie down in green pastures,' " I recited. " 'He leadeth me beside the still waters,' " she said. " 'He restoreth my soul,' " I continued. " ' He leadeth me in the paths of righteousness for his name's sake,' " she said, completing the verse. And so on to the end of the Psalm. No sooner had I recited half of a verse than she would immediately complete it. When I had finished reading the Psalm we bowed our heads in prayer and I asked that God's peace might come into the heart of His servant, that her distress and anxiety might be alleviated. When the prayer was finished she was calmer and more relaxed. Her son, the physician, who had witnessed what had just transpired, was deeply moved and said:

"This is the first time in years that I have seen mother look and act like her old self."

The ministrations of religion on many other occasions have brought comfort and peace to this mother's heart. She has experienced no marked advance in secular knowledge and understanding, but has unfailingly responded to a spiritual ministry.

I am well aware that mental patients sometimes develop very serious and distressing delusions on the subject of religion, as they do on practically every other subject. Nevertheless, in in-

[14] Psalm XXIII.

stances where there has been a previously existing experience of religion, its ministrations can oftentimes reach beyond the barriers of mental conflicts and delusions and bring a measure of peace to a sadly disoriented mind.

The pastor who ministers to individuals, whether it be those who come to his study for an interview or the sick in homes and hospitals, will find himself constantly utilizing spiritual forces greater than he can fully understand or explain. His unfailing ally is prayer. Prayer puts at his disposal inexhaustible resources of spiritual power. It keeps normal people normal, makes possible the solution of personal problems, restores the sick, and comforts the dying.

Oftentimes he will need to teach those who come to him how to pray. Many people, even among professing Christians, think of prayer only in terms of petition. They never get beyond childhood's understanding of prayer. Their prayers are like a child's letter to Santa Claus—they are made up of a series of requests usually for temporal blessings. They appear to be unaware that their deepest needs are spiritual.

Again, it never occurs to them that listening to God is as important a part of prayer as speaking to Him. The boy Samuel in the temple said:

"Speak; for thy servant heareth."[15]

But they reverse the order of the prophet's words and say, in effect, "Listen, Lord, for thy servant speaketh."

In his ministrations, both to people who come to the church for interviews and those whom he visits in their homes, the pastor will find that silent prayer will do much to bring quietness and peace into fevered hearts and lives. Oftentimes, too, when a parishioner finds it exceedingly difficult to come to the point of confessing some wrong-doing, if the pastor will say, "Let us bow our heads for a little time in silent prayer," quiet waiting in the presence of God will awaken the spirit of contrition in the

[15] I Samuel III:10.

heart of his parishioner and oftentimes before the silent prayer is ended he will pour forth a confession from a burdened heart.

The pastor will have to teach his parishioners also that they must *wait* upon God in prayer. The Prophet Isaiah says:

> "They that wait upon the Lord shall renew their strength."[16]

The Psalmist, speaking out of a similar experience, says:

> "Wait on the Lord: be of good courage, and he shall strengthen thine heart: wait, I say, on the Lord."[17]

Most people are accustomed to confine their prayers to a period of three or four minutes. The pastor who has himself known something of the reality of prayer will teach his parishioners to wait upon God, to spend occasionally at least half an hour in His presence, choosing some quiet place and centering the mind upon a passage of Scripture. There he will wait in complete relaxation for the strength of God to flow into his soul, restoring not it alone but his body and mind as well.

But chiefly the pastor will teach his people that receiving is as vital a part of prayer as asking. Many people are disappointed with prayer because it seems to be of little avail. The truth is that they have not been prepared to accept the answer to their own prayers.

I visited a parishioner who was seriously ill of angina pectoris. He was kept alive by inhalations at various intervals of oxygen gas. He was for years an active member of the church and had been known for a long time as a stalwart Christian. With the onset of illness, however, he seemed to have lost completely his grip upon himself and his hold upon his faith. He was in a veritable panic.

When I reached his home and before I went up to the sickroom his wife took me into the living-room and told me that her husband had completely lost his nerve. From time to time he had violent attacks of the heart trouble and some of the

---

[16] Isaiah XL:31.
[17] Psalms XXVII:14.

spasms were so distressing that, in the paroxysm of pain, he tore the skin of his breast with his nails. He lived in constant dread of the next attack.

When I went up to his bedroom I received a warm welcome from my parishioner. His face gave unmistakable evidence of the strain that for weeks he had been under. I was the first person, apart from the members of his family, who was allowed to see him. The doctor had confided in me that there was little chance of his patient's recovery. I moved a chair to the side of the sick man's bed. Immediately he reached out a trembling hand and, catching hold of mine, said:

"I've been through a terrible ordeal and I live in constant fear of another attack. Look at what it does to me," he said, baring his breast and showing me the marks that his nails had made. But that's not the worst. It is this constant fear day and night."

"What are you afraid of?" I asked him, quietly.

"I'm afraid of the next attack," he said. I'm afraid of the pain and I'm afraid of death. I have always been a Christian man. Why should I be afraid like this? I don't know what's happened, what has come over me. I feel like the disciples did on the sea of Galilee, only somehow the Master doesn't seem to be near *me* to bring comfort and peace."

I said to him, "The question you asked me a moment ago is very much like the question Jesus asked His disciples. You said to me, 'Why am I afraid?' and Jesus said to the disciples, 'Why are ye so fearful?' "

"Well, what's the answer?" he said, eagerly. "Can you tell me?"

Immediately there came to my mind a suggestion from a sentence or two of Franz Alexander, referred to by Freud: If one has two dreams in the same night, the former dream may be the key to the interpretation of the latter or the latter to the former. Ought not the same thing to be true of questions? Oftentimes when two questions are asked, one may be the complement of the other. Seldom is one question complete in itself. Pondering this matter in my mind, I said to my parishioner:

"Do you remember the other question that Jesus asked? Were there not two questions?"

"Yes," said the sick man. "He said, 'Why are ye so fearful?' And then, 'How is it that ye have no faith?' "

"If you think about that second question," I said to him, "you will find in it the answer to the first question that Jesus asked His disciples and also to the question which you have just asked me."

"I see what you mean," he said. "I'm afraid because I lack faith. But I can't understand what's the matter with me. I have prayed every day, but I don't get an answer to my prayers."

"What have you requested in your prayers?" I asked him.

"I have asked God to take away my fears and to give me peace of mind," he said.

"You have asked God for this blessing," I told him, "but have you been ready to accept the answer to your own prayers?"

I opened his Bible, which lay on a table at the bedside, and asked him to read a verse that I indicated, and this is what he read:

> " 'All things, whatsoever ye shall ask in prayer, believing, ye shall receive.' "[18]

"I know you have been asking God to help you," I said to him, "but you have lacked the faith to believe that God was ready and willing to answer your prayers. You have not accepted the answer when He is ready to give it to you. You have been holding out your hands and saying: 'Please God, please God, help me. Take away my fear. Give me peace of mind.' You have been straining and agonizing about it and all the while God has been saying to you: 'Hear, my child, take the gift. I have heard your prayer. Accept my peace.' But you have kept on saying, 'Please God, please God, give me peace,' clamouring for the answer that God even in that moment was offering you."

"You are suggesting then that receiving is as much a part of prayer as asking, aren't you?"

"Yes, that is it exactly. We have not only to ask God for His

[18] St. Matthew XXI:22.

blessings, but we have to receive the gifts that He freely offers. When you sent for me today so urgently and when you put out your hand to me as I arrived, both acts were part of your prayer, for you believed that God would use me to bring you peace. You have been asking God to deliver you from fear and to give you peace." "Yes," he responded, "I desperately need God's help." "Are you ready now to accept these blessings which for weeks you have been asking of Him?"

He said: "I am ready now."

I suggested that, instead of continuing to ask God for the blessings he so greatly desired, he should now thank Him for these gifts that God was even now offering to him.

"You pray," I said to him.

From force of long-established habit he started to pray: "O God, give me freedom from fear and give me peace." Then he stammered, hesitated a moment, and commenced again, with increasing confidence:

"O God, I thank Thee that Thou art giving me freedom from fear. I thank Thee for the peace, Thy peace, that I am accepting now. Gratefully I receive Thy gifts. I have needed them so badly. I take them now. I thank Thee, God, for this wonderful blessing."

The silence that followed was quieting and peaceful. I concluded the period of prayer, both audible and silent, with a few words of thanksgiving for the deliverance that had been given to this child of God.

When the prayer was concluded there was already a look of peace on his face and the greater part of the tension and strain had passed.

"That is the first time in my life that I have ever accepted an answer to my own prayers, and think of it, I have been a Bible-class teacher for years! Now I can see what the Master meant when, in his great acts of healing, He said to people:

'As thou hast believed, so be it done unto thee."
'All things are possible to him that believeth.'
'According to your faith be it unto you.'
'Go thy way; thy faith hath made thee whole.' "

"What method have you used in reading your Bible?" I asked him.

"I make a practice," he replied, "of reading one to three chapters each day. I have read the Bible through in the last two years."

"What do you get out of the Bible when you read it?" I asked him.

"Oh, a great deal!" he said. "The Bible is full of instruction for us."

"How much did you read this morning?" I continued.

"Two chapters," he replied.

"What chapters?" I asked him.

"The first two chapters of second Timothy."

"Tell me," I said, "what did you get out of those two chapters? What message did God give to you this morning?"

"Well," he said, with some hesitation, "I can't just recall any special verse."

"It occurs to me," I said to him, "that you haven't been getting help out of your Bible any more than you have been getting benefit from your prayers. May I suggest that in your devotional reading each morning you do not read either two chapters or even one, but that, before you commence to read where you left off the previous day, you ask yourself, 'What is God's message for me this morning?' and then offer a brief prayer that God will help you to be alert to His will for you. Then read along until you come to a verse that you feel definitely is a word from God to you. Stop right there and let that message search your heart. Now please look at the chapters you were reading this morning. In the first chapter are these words:

" 'For God hath not given us the spirit of fear; but of power, and of love, and of a sound mind.' "[19]

"Isn't it strange?" the sick man said, "I didn't notice that verse when I was reading the chapter."

"Well, you see, you missed the message God had for you this morning. He was telling you right in that chapter that He would

[19] II Timothy 1:7.

deliver you from the spirit of fear and give you power and love and a sound mind."

"That text reads as if it were written just for me," he replied. "I am going to think about those words for the rest of the day."

When I left my parishioner he was no longer nervous and depressed. A new interest had come into his life, a fresh understanding of the meaning of prayer and of the Bible. God had become a living reality to him for the first time in his religious experience. I visited him on a number of occasions during the next six months. The turning-point in his illness came with his better understanding and use of prayer and the Bible. He no longer feared the onset of attacks or the prospects of death, and the fact that he had lost these fears helped to make the attacks more infrequent and of much less severity. His convalescence was continuous, so that nine months later he was able to go to his office for a brief period each day. That was four years ago. He spends now at least five hours a day in his office. Not only has he gained deliverance from a distressing physical malady, but he has also grown spiritually and now possesses that for which he had so often prayed—serenity of spirit and inner peace.

In his ministry to the sick there is another point at which the pastor can render signal service, and at which he can demonstrate convincingly to physicians his coöperation with them. I refer to the help which the pastor gives to the sick and their families in that dread hour in which the physician says, "There is nothing more that medical science can do. The case is hopeless." The doctor does not break the news abruptly to the patient or to his family. By quiet hints and suggestions he has already prepared their minds for the final announcement. Oftentimes both patients and their families demand an explicit answer to the question, "Doctor, is there any hope of recovery?"

There are infrequent instances, of course, where the doctor is mistaken in his assertion that the case is hopeless. In such instances, as well as in all others, the pastor, by awakening the patient's faith in the healing power of God, will supplement the efforts of the doctor to bring about his recovery instead of abandoning the patient to one of the modern healing cults with their perilous disregard of the God-given resources of modern medicine.

The pastor who is faithful and competent in his sick visitations makes it clear to the patient and his family that the Christian who believes in God and makes intelligent and faithful use of the Bible and prayer has available to him every resource of spiritual value possessed by any healing cult in the world. There would be fewer of these cults in existence today if churches and pastors engaged more faithfully in their ministries to the sick and if physicians were more alert to the fact that treating the whole of each patient includes not only the healing of the body but also of the mind and of the soul.

It is not my purpose at this time to deal any further with these extremely few cases where a wrong diagnosis has been made, but rather with the more familiar instance where a patient's condition is hopeless beyond all possibility of error.

I had been visiting a member of my parish for some months. She was ill of what was first believed to be a simple digestive disorder. Then followed further examinations and X-rays. One day her doctor stopped me on the street and said: "I have a very difficult job ahead of me. I must tell her family that these is no slightest hope of her recovery. It will not be easy, because they have not suspected that her illness is serious and they mean so very much to each other."

I asked the doctor if he would let me know when he was ready to break the news to the family, as I wanted to be with them, too. A few days later, while we were all gathered in the living-room, the doctor came down from the sick-room and quietly announced the sad news to the family. They stood up bravely under the crushing blow. Shortly the physician left and I talked with them of their faith in God and of the consolation and strength that He would give to them. The husband wondered whether his wife would be able to retain her courage and faith. "She loves life so much," he said, "and she is so wrapped up in her family. I don't know how she will take this when she finds out that she cannot recover."

The patient came to suspect the seriousness of her condition and said to the doctor abruptly one day, "There is no hope of my getting better, is there Doctor? I want you to tell me the truth." Very gently and kindly he said to her, "I am afraid that is the truth, but I am going to do my best to keep you comfortable. I am going to stand by you constantly. You have an excellent nurse and a devoted family. You have something else that many patients do not have; that is, your faith. Keep that aglow."

That evening, I had a long conversation with the dying woman. I read to her the promise of God to His people:

> " 'But now thus saith the Lord, . . . Fear not: for I have redeemed thee, I have called thee by thy name; thou art mine. When thou passest through the waters, I will be with thee; and through the rivers, they shall not overflow thee: . . . For I am the Lord thy God, the Holy One of Israel, thy Saviour.' "[20]

I assured her that just as truly as God was with His children in days of old, guiding them through the perilous waters, so He would be with her in the Great Adventure upon which she was soon to set forth. I talked to her of Jesus' assurance[21] that Eternal Life is a fellowship with God so rich and so personal that death is powerless to break it; that He who had been the Companion of her pilgrimage heretofore would be with her to the end of the journey.

She eagerly laid hold of the promises of the Bible, and with serene and untroubled faith awaited the end. Over and over again she would ask me to repeat to her the words of her favourite text:

> "But now thus saith the Lord, . . . Fear not: for I have redeemed thee, I have called thee by thy name; thou

---

[20] Isaiah XLIII:1, 2, 3.
[21] St. John XVII:3.

art mine. When thou passest through the waters, I will be with thee; and through the rivers, they shall not overflow thee: . . . For I am the Lord thy God, the Holy One of Israel, thy Saviour."

Each time, as I concluded it, her face lighted up and she said, "I know that He will be with me."

One day, after I had returned from a visit to a neighbouring city, I went at once to this parishioner's home. The father and the two daughters met me at the door. I was somewhat surprised when they led me into the living-room instead of taking me directly upstairs, as they had been accustomed to do. After a moment, the husband said, with deep emotion:

"There is no use in your going up to see my wife. She is unconscious. She slipped into a coma during the night and has not recognized any of us all day long. The doctor was in and he says that the end will come in an hour or two."

The two daughters were red-eyed and weeping. One of them said, "If she could only have given us some word or sign that everything was well with her, it would have made it easier for us."

It was then five o'clock in the afternoon of a winter's day. The shadows were already gathering in the room. I turned to the husband and said:

"I would like to go up in any case to see your wife and to offer a word of prayer." I signalled for him and his daughters to accompany me. We found the nurse standing beside the bed in watchful silence. "Have you spoken to your wife today?" I asked her husband. "Yes, all of us have; the girls, the nurse, and I, but we have not been able to get any response from her. We tried again just a few minutes before you came in."

I drew a chair up to the bedside where her right hand was extended outside the bed-clothes. Taking her hand in mine, I repeated slowly the words of the text that she had learned to love:

"'But now thus saith the Lord, . . . Fear not: for I have redeemed thee, I have called thee by thy name; thou art mine. When thou passest through the waters, I will be with thee; and through the rivers, they shall not overflow thee: . . . For I am the Lord thy God, the Holy One of Israel, thy Saviour.' "

As I reached the closing words of the passage I discerned some slight evidence of consciousness in the flickering of the sick woman's eyelids. We all started forward eagerly. It appeared as if she were rousing from her comatose state. I commenced to repeat the text in a firm tone:

"But now thus saith the Lord, . . . Fear not: for I have redeemed thee, I have called thee by thy name; thou art mine. . . ."

I had reached the end of the third line when the sick woman's eyes slowly opened and she joined me in the words:

"When thou passest through the waters, I will be with thee . . ."

continuing to recite the whole passage to its close. Her lips framed the words softly, but everyone around the bed could hear them distinctly. And then she added slowly, in a voice that was faint but yet audible to us all, "He . . . is . . . with . . . me."

Instantly one of the daughters, bending over her, said, "You know us, mother, don't you?" Her answer was a smile of recognition and of ineffable peace as she slipped into unconsciousness again. Within an hour's time she had passed away. . . . And as John Bunyan said of another pilgrim who had crossed the self-same river: all the trumpets sounded for her on the other side.

Here is but one more illustration of the fact that spiritual stimulation can reach out and touch the soul and, through the soul, the mind and body, long after secular stimulation has ceased to reach the inner citadels of the individual's life. It should awaken us all to a realization of the power of the energies of the spirit.

In this chapter I have dealt almost wholly with individuals whom I visited in their homes, all of whom were members of one or other of my parishes. In previous chapters I have told of my interviews with individuals, a percentage of whom were not members of my congregation.

More than 60 per cent of all the interviews which I conduct at my church are with members of my own congregation. Between 30 and 40 per cent are people who have happened into a service or who have heard my addresses over the radio. These, too, I have described as parishioners, for a minister's work cannot be circumscribed by the limits of his own parish. A great Christian minister of another century said, "The world is my parish," and there is a sense in which that is true of every minister.

The physician of souls includes in his ministry all classes and conditions of men—the high and the low, the rich and the poor, the old and the young—irrespective of their rank or station in life. He deals with all who come to him in the spirit of sympathetic understanding, friendliness, trust, and love. Never by word or sign does he indicate that any of the confidences that have been given to him have hurt or shocked him. Instantly he puts himself in the other person's place, and realizes the difficulties that he or she is facing because he has first known himself. Whatever confidences are given to him he receives in the spirit of sympathetic understanding. It is not his task to judge people. He is here to serve them as a minister of Christ.

He is friendly to those who come to him seeking his help. It is too easy for ministers as it is for doctors to become professional in their manner of dealing with people, to regard them as "cases," to forget that they are souls. Nothing will drive people from them so quickly and render them incapable of helping individuals as the spirit of unfriendliness.

He trusts those who come to him. He lets them know that he believes in them, in the possibilities of good latent in them. Oftentimes the people who come to consult a minister have lost faith in themselves as well as in God and their fellow-men.

Trust and confidence on his part in them will awaken their self-confidence.

Finally he will have a consuming love for souls. The man who does not love men and women, who is contemptuous or cynical of them, has no place in the Christian ministry or in any other profession where he must meet and deal with individuals. Jesus linked in equal importance love of our neighbour with love of God. He that truly loves God will love his fellow-men. We are never more Godlike than when our hearts are moved with sympathy, compassion, and love for our fellow-men. It was the disciple who leaned on Jesus' bosom who wrote:

> "Beloved, let us love one another: for love is of God; and every one that loveth is born of God, and knoweth God.
>
> He that loveth not knoweth not God; for God is love . . . he that dwelleth in love dwelleth in God, and God in him."[22]

The human heart that receives and expresses the love of God is a heart at peace. The pastor who would be a true physician of souls will himself dwell in the love and peace of God. If those who come to him with their problems and their needs find that the minister is unsympathetic, nervous, lacking in serenity and poise, sympathy, and love, they will not bring their problems to him. Rather will they go away saying, "Physician, heal thyself." Therefore, nothing else is of such importance to the physician of souls as his own inner life, his own knowledge and experience of God. He who himself is living the abundant life is able to lead others into it. He who himself has the peace of God brings it to others. He himself is a living example of what faith in God can do for a man. His very presence inspires hope and confidence, and radiates spiritual power.

The physician of souls seeks above all else to bring people to God. Whether they be normal people desirous of continuing normal, sinful people bearing on their hearts a burden of guilt unconfessed and unforgiven, fearful people living amid a nightmare of abnormal anxieties, unhappy people caught in a tangle

[22] I John IV:7, 8, 16.

of unsolved problems or untamed passions, or even little children who, because of wrong training or bad environment, have formed behavior patterns that, uncorrected, will mar their happiness through life, each and all of these the physician of souls brings to God, where fretted lives find restoration and peace. Ministers without knowledge of psychiatry and with a strong faith in God have worked effectively with individuals, but he truly is a physician of souls who brings to each individual coming to him for help not only all the knowledge and experience that he can glean from the physicians of the mind but also an experiential knowledge of the healing and transforming power of God.

Acknowledgments

The author wishes to express his appreciation to the following authors and publishers for their generous permission to quote from their copyrighted works:

To W. W. Norton and Company, Inc., for quotations from *The Neurotic Personality of Our Time*, by Dr. Karen Horney.

To The Christian Century for quotation from an article entitled "Betraying the Confessional," by Frances J. Nickels.

To Doubleday, Doran and Company, Inc., for quotation from *The Conquest of Fear*, by Basil King, copyright 1921.

To D. Appleton-Century Company, Inc., for quotations from *Child Guidance*, by Smiley Blanton, B.S., M.D., and Margaret Gray Blanton, and *Freedom in the Modern World*, by John MacMurray.

To Robert M. McBride and Company for quotation from *Psychology and Morals*, by J. A. Hadfield.

To John Wiley and Sons, Inc., for quotation from *Manual of Psychiatry*, by Aaron J. Rosanoff, M.D.

To Charles Scribner's Sons for quotation from *Psychiatry and Mental Health*, by John Rathbone Oliver.

To Alfred A. Knopf, Inc., for stanza from "Sand and Foam," by Kahlil Gibran.

To Garden City Publishing Company, Inc., for illustration from *Understanding Human Nature*, by Alfred Adler.

To Ives Washburn, Inc., for quotations from *Let's Be Normal*, by Fritz Künkel.

To Harcourt, Brace and Company, Inc., for quotation from *Modern Man in Search of a Soul*, by C. G. Jung.

To Harper & Brothers for quotations from The Holy Bible: A New Translation by James Moffatt.

INDEX